Unraveled

A Journey from Breakdown to Breakthrough

Vanessa France

Grace & Light Press

Unraveled: A Journey from Breakdown to Breakthrough By Vanessa France

Copyright © 2025 by Vanessa France

All rights reserved. No part of this book may be reproduced, stored in a retrieval system, or transmitted in any form or by any means – electronic, mechanical, photocopying, recording, or otherwise – without prior written permission of the publisher, except in the case of brief quotations embodied in critical reviews and certain other noncommercial uses permitted by copyright law.

First Edition

ISBN Print: 979-8-9930743-0-6

ISBN e-book: 979-8-9930743-1-3, eBook v1.0.2

Published by Grace & Light Press

Printed in the United States of America

For Matt, Maddie, Lali, Cam & Jack

You are the reason I kept going.
You are the light I reached for in the dark.

Matt – your steady love, your quiet strength, your belief in me even when I couldn't believe in myself... it anchored me. Thank you for standing beside me through every broken piece and every slow rebuild. For standing strong when I was falling apart. For never walking away.

Maddie, Lali, Cam & Jack – my four amazing children.
You are my heart, my why, my greatest teachers.

This story was never just mine.
It was the story of how I learned to come home to myself... so I could show up fully for all of you.

I love you all more than every word in these pages.

Sometimes we have to come undone

to find the threads that lead us home.

Table of Contents

Foreword   1

Introduction   3

1. The Aisle Seat   5
2. Side By Side   9
3. Control   13
4. The Trade   19
5. Damage, Rearranged   24
6. The Beautiful Mess   28
7. The Space He Left   33
8. When Jack Arrived   37
9. The Gift of Returning   43
10. When The World Fell Apart   47
11. The Climb   54
12. Feeling It All   63
13. Beginning Again   67
14. Learning to Stay   73
15. The Mat That Carried Me Home   77
16. Answering The Call   84

17. The Messy, Miraculous Middle	90
18. Anchored in Faith	95
19. Wired This Way	100
20. Let Go	105
Afterword	109
Acknowledgements	110
Resources & Further Reading	115
Reader Reflection	117
Notes	119
About The Author	125

Foreword

By Teresa Coyle Airey, IBCLC, CD(DONA), CBS, CBE

I met the author, Vanessa, during a time when parents often find themselves evaluating who they are and what kind of messages they want to pass on to their children.

Unraveled is an honest and brave look into the life of a mom who holds it all together for her societal role – but who is dangerously destructive to her personal self through addiction. This sincere memoir weaves a riveting account of finding oneself at the edge and searching for the courage and strength to gain back a life that is honest, forgiving, and whole.

Author Vanessa France fully captures the raw and tangled feelings that represent both the struggles and the joys of parenthood – and how they coincide with finding your way back home to yourself, to the things you love, and to the ones who love you. I am forever grateful that our paths crossed and honored to recommend this book to anyone who has ever thought, *There must be more in this life for me.*

Unraveled is a lesson in love – love for yourself, for the things that make you unique, and for returning to the best version of yourself. This book is an inspiration for all. Beautifully written, it embodies the essence of what truly matters in a lifetime.

VANESSA FRANCE

Teresa Coyle Airey, IBCLC, CD(DONA), CBS, CBE
Owner & Founder, *Peaceful Birth and Beyond Services*
North Central Massachusetts

Bio: Teresa is, first and foremost, a mother to four grown children and a grandmother to five little ones whom she adores. She has worked with families for close to four decades as an International Board-Certified Lactation Consultant, Lactation Educator, Childbirth Educator, and Birth & Postpartum Doula. Teresa works intimately with families in the childbearing years and has supported and counseled thousands during the tender times of growth and change.

Introduction

For most of my life, I thought healing would begin at a dramatic turning point, at a rock bottom followed by a rise. But it didn't start that way for me.

My healing began not with a leap forward but with a look back. Back to a frightened little girl on a cross-country flight, clutching a plastic toy airplane like her life depended on it. Back to the moment my body first screamed what I didn't yet have the language to say: *I am not okay.*

That moment didn't just mark the beginning of anxiety. It marked the beginning of silence. Of disappearing. Of perfection. It was the first thread in a lifelong unraveling – of trying to hold it all together even as, piece by piece, I came undone.

This isn't just a memoir about addiction or anxiety or motherhood. It's a story about what happens when we spend our lives trying to be good, quiet, and small – and the courage it takes to stop performing and start telling the truth. It's about the winding road from bulimia to blackout, from control to surrender, from losing myself to finally finding my way back.

And somewhere along that path, I found a mat – a simple rectangle of space that became my sanctuary. A place to breathe. To fall apart. To come home. The mat didn't fix everything. But it held me while I healed. It gave me space to feel what I had spent decades trying to outrun. Letting go, I learned, isn't weakness. Instead, it is holy. It is brave. And it's where the real story begins.

VANESSA FRANCE

This isn't a story tied up in a bow. It's not a straight line from broken to healed. It's a story about unraveling and weaving myself back together again and again – in moments of loss, in the face of addiction, in the sacred, messy beauty of motherhood. It's about coming home to my body, my breath, my faith.

If you've ever tried to outrun your pain, to shrink yourself into something more lovable, to smile through the ache – this story is for you. Because here's what I know now: we all carry stories that deserve to be told. We all hold value that can help someone else feel less alone. And when we share those stories – raw, imperfect, and true – we create space for healing. Not just for ourselves, but for each other.

So, come with me. Take my hand. We'll go back. We'll go deep.

And then – let's stop holding it all together and let go. We'll see it was never the end.

The unraveling is where the story truly begins.

Chapter One

The Aisle Seat

"*Sweetheart... It's okay. You're okay. You're safe, I promise.*"

My voice is slow and steady – low and warm, like golden honey stirred into hot tea. I crouch beside the narrow seat, close enough to touch the frayed armrest of the airplane chair, close enough to feel the tremble of fear radiating from the small girl curled tightly into herself, clutching a plastic toy airplane like it might hold the whole world together.

Her breath is shallow, her blonde hair disheveled from frantic crying, sticking to her damp, tear-streaked cheeks in tangled strands. Her small frame curls into the seat, shaking, as she grips tightly to the toy airplane. It was meant to be a souvenir – something handed out by flight attendants to calm young travelers and spark wonder. But for her, it isn't a toy. It's a lifeline. A tether to something solid in a world that suddenly feels like it might vanish beneath her.

"You're not alone," I whisper. "I know it feels scary. Your heart is racing, your hands are shaking, and everything around you feels too loud, too fast. But listen to me: this feeling? It's just a feeling. It can't hurt you. It will pass."

She sobs harder, the sound broken and jagged, too big for her tiny body. Passengers nearby shift uneasily in their seats – one lets out a sigh, another casts a quick glance, someone murmurs something under their breath. The words aren't cruel, but they land like a slap. And just like that, her fear is joined by something else: shame. The awareness of being watched. Of taking up too much space. Of being too much. Her blotchy, tear-streaked face turns, searching the aisle. Her legs dangle off the seat, feet swinging in wild, anxious rhythm. She isn't looking for adventure. She's looking for someone to rescue her. Someone to explain. Someone to hold her. Someone to make it stop.

But no one comes.

Next to her, tucked against the window, is another little girl, just a year or so older, but trying hard to wear the role of protector. She doesn't cry. She doesn't move. She stares ahead, frozen, doing her best to be brave. But she's just a child too – quietly holding her breath.

I turn my attention back to the younger girl, crouching closer. "Close your eyes," I tell her, my voice softer now, gentler. "Picture something warm. Sunlight shining on your face. The softness of your favorite blanket at home. The sound of the ocean. Feel your breath go in... and then out. Like ocean waves. You're okay. You're safe. You are so, so brave. Braver than you know."

Still, no response. Her tiny hands remain locked around the toy plane, clinging to it like it might somehow carry her home. But it's like she can't hear me, can't see me – like I'm not even there.

And in a way... I'm not.

Because that little girl... is me.

And I wasn't safe. Not then. Not really. I was only four years old, on my first flight, flying with my sister across the country – more than 2,000 miles from home – to visit our father who no longer lived with us. Children of divorce, sent into the sky alone. No mother. No father. No familiar hand to hold. No soothing voice to explain why my heart felt like it might burst, why I couldn't breathe, why I felt like I was floating outside of my body.

That day, somewhere high above the clouds, I had my first panic attack. It's the first real memory of my life. No one knew what it was – not the flight attendants, not my sister, not the other passengers. Not even me. There wasn't a name for it in my world yet – just a quiet chaos unraveling inside a small girl holding on for dear life.

I'm forty-seven now. A mother of four. A woman who has spent decades unlearning what fear taught me. Untangling the silence. Trying to speak the words I never knew how to say.

It was my therapist who gave me the assignment that brought me back here. "Go back," she said. "Find her. Speak to the little girl inside you. Tell her what she needed to hear that day."

So I did.

What I didn't expect was how that simple assignment would open a door. I've always been clearer on the page than out loud – speaking, I second-guess; writing, I hear myself. Sitting with a pen – later a blinking cursor – the noise fell away and something steady came through. That homework became pages; the pages became this book.

This is where my story begins.

Not with sobriety. Not with a rock bottom. Not with becoming a mother. Not even with healing. But here. In the aisle seat of a commercial jet 30,000 feet in the air, with a heart that didn't yet have the language to say *I'm scared*.

Because that fear didn't end when the wheels touched down. It followed me. Quietly. Persistently. It crept into my childhood, shaped my teenage years, tiptoed alongside my adult years, and shadowed my motherhood – not just in thoughts and feelings, but in the way my body moved, held tension, and flared with pain I couldn't explain. It wore disguises. It learned to speak fluently in perfectionism, in control, in silence. It turned into disordered eating. Into alcohol dependence. Into shame.

It told me: *Hold it together. Be good. Be quiet. Don't need too much.*

And I listened.

I didn't understand the feeling for years. I didn't have the vocabulary for panic, trauma, or what it meant to dissociate. But the tight chest? The buzzing thoughts? The desperate need to be held and the unbearable fear of being seen? That part never really left me. It just changed shape.

Now, after all this time, after decades of trying to make sense of it all, I finally get to go back. To find her. To kneel beside her. To say what no one said that day:

You're not broken. You were never broken. You are safe now. And I'm not going anywhere.

And the most extraordinary part?

For the first time in my life – I believe it.

Chapter Two

Side By Side

From the very beginning, it was me and my sister – two little girls trying to find steady ground in a world that kept shifting beneath us. Marriages came and went. Last names changed. New homes, new step-parents, new step-siblings, and new sets of rules. But through it all, we had each other. Our mom did her best through seasons that weren't easy – moving, stretching what little we had, trying to keep us steady. What never wavered was the bond my sister and I carried between us.

We fought like sisters do, especially being so close in age – sharing clothes, sharing space, but trying to carve out some sense of independence while living right on top of each other. Sometimes we shared a bedroom. Sometimes a bed. And sometimes, we'd scream at each other one minute and be curled up watching a movie together the next.

But the truth is, she was my rock. She always had been. Even on that plane when we were just little girls – alone in the sky, she was steady. Stoic. Calm in a way I couldn't be. I remember shaking with panic, clutching that toy plane, and looking at her beside me. She wasn't crying. She wasn't falling apart. And just knowing she was there made me believe, somehow, I would survive it, too.

That's how it always was. Things felt complicated for me in ways they didn't for her. Not just emotionally – although that was part of it – but physically, too. My joints ached when they shouldn't have. There were times when things felt loose or out of place, but no one could quite explain why. As a baby, I had to wear a metal hip brace to help realign my joints – something stiff, cold and clanky that had to be put on before I slept. My mother used to wonder if it was because she carried me on her hip too much while chasing my sister around. But no one really knew.

And then came the strange circulation issues. My fingers and toes would go numb out of nowhere, turning white as snow, then purplish-blue, then an angry, pulsing red as the blood returned. It was painful in a strange, stinging way – like tiny needles were waking up under my skin. The episodes came often, especially in the cold, or if I was even slightly stressed. My sister and I would try to frantically rub warmth back into my hands, blow on them, anything to bring them back to life. It was unnerving, especially as a kid, to see your body do something no one else around you seemed to understand. Eventually, the doctors named it: Raynaud's. Annoying, but manageable, they said. Wear gloves. Avoid triggers. Learn to live with it.

Not long after, something new began to happen – something that scared me in a different way. My heart started racing and fluttering in a way I couldn't explain. I would end up in a cardiologist's office, electrodes stuck to my chest, my breath held while the machines tried to capture the irregular rhythm that had become a constant background hum. Mitral valve prolapse, they finally diagnosed. Not serious, they said. Just something to monitor. Something to live with. I'd need antibiotics before dental visits to protect my heart. Just another strange footnote in a growing list of medical oddities that made me feel different.

In middle school, it was my knee. Sharp, relentless pain that made it hard to run, to jump, to play. Basketball, which I loved, became harder to keep up with. Eventually, surgery was the next step – the fix that was supposed to make it all better. It didn't. Not really. And I remember my sister there afterward – steady as ever – helping me get settled on the couch, bringing snacks, watching music videos on MTV with me, Doritos and a Coke balanced on my lap, my leg propped up. We didn't talk about the pain. She didn't ask many questions. She was just there. And somehow, that said everything.

On top of all of that were the relentless stomach issues I could never explain. Bloating, pain, discomfort that never seemed to follow a pattern. No diagnosis, no relief. Just the constant hum of unease in my body, like something was always slightly off. It made me feel fragile. Different. Like my body was a puzzle no one could solve.

Each issue came with its own specialist. My mom and I would sit in new waiting rooms – only to receive another set of vague answers and follow-up appointments. Another folder filled with paperwork, diagrams, and a quiet shrug from someone in a white coat: "You'll just have to learn to live with this." And I tried. I always tried. I felt like somehow all of these issues were my fault.

But what no one seemed to name – at least not at first – was the thread running through it all. The thing that wasn't listed on the scans or spelled out in lab results. Anxiety. Not loud. Not dramatic. Just constant. A steady ache beneath it all, like static you eventually forget is there until you realize it's been shaping the way you breathe, the way you react, the way you live.

I began collecting terms – panic attacks, anxiety, sensitivity. No one could quite name it, and I didn't know how to explain it. But I knew something inside me wasn't working the way it was supposed to. The language helped a little – it gave shape to what I was feeling, made it feel less invisible. But still, without a clear diagnosis or a concrete plan, I often wondered if people truly understood. If they saw how hard it really was. The guidance, though, remained the same: learn to live with it.

None of these things were considered serious, not exactly. Not life-threatening. Not dramatic enough to draw real concern. But they were chronic. Lingering. Unresolved. And I internalized all of them. I learned to minimize, to apologize, to downplay. To say "I'm fine" even when I wasn't. To feel like a burden for even bringing it up. Because when you have a bunch of things wrong, but no one can really name what's wrong, you start to wonder if maybe you are the problem. That maybe you're just too much. Too sensitive. Too needy. Too dramatic. Too... something.

I carried it all quietly – like a weight I didn't have permission to set down. And through it all, my sister was there. Even when we were in different phases of life. Even when time and distance stretched between us. Even when the words were missing. She remained the constant – the one who knew the whole story. The one who saw the scared little girl behind the brave face.

It would take years before I learned that the pain I had been compartmentalizing wasn't a collection of separate issues, but a single, tangled thread. That it wasn't just in my head. That there was a name for what I had been carrying all along. But back then, I did what I had always done: I kept going. I smiled. I pretended everything was fine.

But I wasn't alone. Because no matter how heavy the world felt, my sister was always there – steady beside me. Side by side. Two girls growing up in a world full of chaos and curveballs – holding on to each other, and to whatever steadiness we could find.

Chapter Three

Control

Despite the ache, there were seasons that felt almost magical – warm, bright, and untouched by anything heavy.

There were summers that still feel golden in my memory – long, sun-drenched days camping in our Volkswagen camper with my mom and stepdad. The air smelled of campfire and toasted marshmallows, and time didn't matter. My sister and I rode bikes down winding dirt roads, played paddleball with my mom until our arms were sore and our cheeks ached from smiling, and fell asleep sticky with lake water and sugar, stars scattered across the sky like confetti.

After we moved back up north, we'd also visit Nana at her lake house – not our grandmother by blood, but by bond. Hazel, though we only ever called her Nana, once moved all the way from New Hampshire to Florida to help care for us while Mom worked full-time to get back on her feet. Her home smelled of mothballs and orange peels and always felt safe. She sang along to Elvis on her 8-track tapes, scooped Neapolitan ice cream into cones, then carefully licked each into shape before handing them to us with a wink. She ended her sentences with "and that," a phrase we barely noticed then but repeat now with affection – a thread that still ties us back to her.

Those moments live in me too – the softness, the laughter, the lightness of being little and barefoot and free.

And yet, even in those golden years, there was a quiet undercurrent – a sense that things around us were shifting, unpredictable. My sister and I learned how to read a room, how to steady ourselves when things felt tense. We became each other's anchor, bonded not only by joy but by learning how to navigate the edges.

By my teenage years, that skill had turned into something else entirely – a quiet internal pressure that never let up. On the outside, I was the responsible daughter, the strong student, the athlete who seemed fine. On the inside, I was holding my breath.

Anxiety no longer screamed. It whispered: *be good, be quiet, be small, be easy to love.* While that pressure built, the world around me reinforced its own expectations. I had just entered high school – a time when everything already felt uncertain and exposed. Looking back now, I realize how loud the cultural noise was – and how deeply it sank in.

It was the 90s – an era that glorified thinness. Everywhere we turned, the message was impossible to miss: *smaller was better.* It didn't matter how thin you already were – it was never enough. Magazine covers shouted about weight loss. Commercials praised fat-free everything. Grocery aisles overflowed with diet versions of the foods we used to love. Even the fine print admitted harm – I remember staring at a bag of chips that warned "Contains olestra. May cause abdominal cramping and loose stools... anal leakage." How could something that literally hurt our bodies be acceptable? The answer was clear: if it kept us thin, the pain was worth it.

That messaging sank in deep. It taught me that worth was conditional – that to be loved, I had to be less.

As if the pressure of the 90s wasn't heavy enough, along came a boy.

He paid attention in a way no one else had. He remembered the small things. He listened. He made me feel chosen – wanted, like I mattered. For a girl who had spent most of her life feeling either too much or not enough, it was intoxicating.

At that age, a relationship like this didn't just mean something – it meant everything. My world began to orbit around him. His attention became my validation. His moods dictated my days.

He was intense. Possessive. Jealous. But to my naïve teenage mind, that didn't feel like a red flag – it felt like passion. Like proof that I was special. The intensity was addictive. I had spent so long wondering what was wrong with me, and now someone wanted me. Needed me. And I clung to that with everything I had.

Everything moved fast. There was no room to pause, to reflect, to ask myself what I wanted. And when I gave him the most sacred part of me – my trust, my body, my first experience of real intimacy – I believed it would seal something in place. That it would settle his insecurity. That it would prove I was his. That it would prove I was enough.

But it didn't bring us closer. It quietly undid something in me.

Because not long after, I found out I hadn't been the only one. While he was reaching for me, he was reaching for others, too – offering pieces of himself I thought were mine alone. The deception hit like a wave I never saw coming. I felt gutted. Exposed. Foolish. But even more painful than what he did was the story I told myself about why: *this happened because you're not enough.*

That lie became the lens I carried into everything that followed. So when the heartbreak came – the lies, the humiliation – I didn't leave him. I stayed. Not because it didn't hurt, but because I believed I had to earn love. Because I didn't believe I deserved better. Because I thought this was what love looked like: painful, confusing, earned.

From there, I turned the pain inward. I told myself that if I had been prettier, thinner, quieter, easier – more like *her* – maybe I would have been enough to keep him honest.

It wasn't just his disloyalty that broke me – it was the way it confirmed the quiet fears already living inside me. Those fears didn't begin with him. They had been planted long before, by a culture that praised girls for taking up less space and taught us our worth was tied to being wanted.

If I was the problem, maybe I could fix me.

I started with my appearance. My wild curly hair once felt like freedom – a little unruly, a little loud, a little me. But after heartbreak, it felt like too much. I smoothed the frizz, straightened the curl, swept it across my forehead to make it look smaller. It wasn't about style. It was about erasure. About reshaping myself into someone more lovable, more acceptable.

Then I turned to my body. I couldn't control him. I couldn't undo the ache. But I could control what I ate. I could control how much space I took up. With high school's comparisons echoing, the culture's demands pressing in, and the ache of his betrayal still raw, I convinced myself that maybe if I needed less, asked for less, became less, I'd be harder to leave. Maybe if I disappeared just a little, I'd finally be enough.

At first, it was subtle. Skipping meals. New rules that made me feel powerful for saying no. Hunger became something to be proud of – a quiet rebellion against a world of feelings I didn't know how to hold.

Then came the flip side. The shame. The moments when I couldn't hold it all together. The binges – quiet, frantic, desperate. Eating like I was trying to fill a void that had no bottom. And afterward, the self-hatred was immediate. Overwhelming. That's when the purging started.

It wasn't something I planned. It began as a desperate attempt to undo what I had eaten, what I had felt, what I couldn't bear to carry. I needed a way to get it out. To empty myself of the shame, the chaos, the need. It wasn't only about the food. It was about the ache underneath it. The sense that I had taken in too much – into my body, into my heart – and didn't know how else to release it.

I didn't know the word bulimia then. I only knew that this ritual made the storm go quiet – if only for a moment. It felt like control. But it wasn't power – it was pain, repackaged as discipline, hidden under the performance of perfection.

I wore that mask well. The smiling, bubbly student. The dependable daughter. The friend who always had it together. No one suspected what I was doing when no one was looking. Not my sister. Not even my mom. At least not at first. Eventually she noticed the signs – the "showers" after meals, the time in the bathroom, the way my body never relaxed. She asked, gently at first, then with concern, later with fear.

But I always had an answer. I was tired. I was stressed. I had a test. *I was fine.*

But I wasn't fine. I was drowning in shame. Afraid that if anyone really saw me, they'd leave too. That if this was who I truly was, no one could love me. Not even me.

VANESSA FRANCE

Looking back now, I can see what I couldn't then: anxiety doesn't always scream. Sometimes it whispers. Sometimes it hides in bathroom tiles and fake smiles. Sometimes it looks like perfection – but underneath, it's fear.

This was the next chapter of my unraveling – the chapter where I tried to eat away the grief, purge the guilt, and perform my way into being enough. The chapter where I longed so deeply to be loved that I erased myself in the process.

That's the trap of control. It whispers safety, but breathes shame. It promises order, but delivers silence. And sometimes, it moves into the body – into quiet rituals, into hunger games, into the ways we try to make ourselves less.

Eating disorders aren't about vanity. They're about pain – a pain so deep it seeks invisibility. And before you even realize it, you're vanishing – not just in size, but in spirit. And the path back feels impossible to reach.

Chapter Four

The Trade

No one really knew.

Not the friends I laughed with at lunch. Not the girls I ran beside on the field hockey team every afternoon – shoulder to shoulder during practice, like we were all carrying the same weight.

But mine was different. It was quieter. Heavier. Hidden.

I never told anyone about the binges. The purging. The constant calculations around food. I never said how most mornings I could barely look at myself in the mirror – how I lived in a loop of restriction and regret. I smiled on cue. I played the part. And then I dragged my tired, aching body from the final bell to the field, still pretending I was fine.

There were afternoons when I could barely focus. My stomach churned, my head throbbed, my limbs felt heavy and disconnected. But I laced up anyway. Showed up anyway. Pushed through anyway – hoping that movement might quiet the chaos in my mind.

Even so, being part of the team gave me something to hold onto. The shared sweat and banter, the post-game bus rides, the sideline cheers – they grounded me in ways I didn't fully understand at the time.

Some days still glow in my memory. After practice, we'd cram into my beat-up 1985 Toyota Celica, windows down, hair damp with sweat, 90s hip hop blasting through the speakers. We'd belt out every lyric, laughing as we cruised the winding back roads, our field hockey sticks rattling in the trunk, the cool air rushing in to meet our flushed skin. For those brief, joy-filled moments, the ache in my body quieted. The world felt light. And I felt like I belonged.

And my coach – she probably never realized it, but her voice, steady and strong, cut through the noise in my head. She expected something of me, and that expectation gave me structure. When I was retreating from the world, my team pulled me back in – simply by letting me be part of theirs.

Those moments held me together for a while. But the ache always returned – deeper, heavier, harder to silence. The rituals I had relied on for control were beginning to fray. I was still restricting, still binging and purging, but it wasn't working the way it used to. My body ached. My mind raced. The pressure to keep up the performance was relentless – good student, good athlete, good daughter, good friend – and I didn't know how much longer I could keep wearing the mask. I was losing my grip. Quietly, but steadily.

And then I found alcohol.

I can't even remember what I drank first – maybe a cheap beer, maybe something mixed with juice – but I do remember exactly how it made me feel. It hit fast, like someone had opened a window in a suffocating room. The tension in my shoulders dissolved. The buzzing in my head quieted. My chest, always tight with fear, loosened. The constant calculations – what to eat, what not to eat, how to speak, how to shrink – suddenly stopped.

For the first time in as long as I could remember, I felt relief. I felt okay in my body. I laughed without overthinking. I spoke without rehearsing. I didn't care what I looked like or whether I was too much or not enough. The weight of being *me* lifted. I felt free.

And underneath that false freedom was something even more seductive: escape.

It didn't just soften the sharp edges of my anxiety – it erased them. It numbed the gnawing hunger, the bruised shame, the constant ache in my stomach and my soul. Alcohol didn't ask anything of me. It didn't demand perfection. It just said *shh* and wrapped itself around me like a warm blanket. And in a world where everything felt too loud, too bright, too much – that silence was intoxicating. It didn't feel dangerous. It felt like a gift.

And that's when the trade began.

I didn't recognize it as a trade at first – one escape swapped for another. There was no conscious decision, no big moment. Just a slow slide into something new. Like wading into the shallow end of a pool that deepens without warning, until your feet can no longer touch the bottom.

Alcohol was easy to find. Beers stolen from the fridge. Half-empty liquor bottles poured into water bottles. There were house parties with barely any supervision – tables lined with Zima, Boone's, Smirnoff Ice, neon-colored bottles of Aftershock with candy crystals clinging to the bottom. And the one with floating gold flakes – like some twisted prize. Eventually, fake IDs that opened the door even wider. Getting my hands on it wasn't the issue. Stopping was.

Because it was never just one drink. Not for me. The moment the warmth hit, my body – my mind – craved more. Always more. One became two. Two became four. A bottle. I chased that feeling, desperate to sustain it. Somewhere deep down, I knew it wasn't normal. But I also didn't care. I just wanted to feel okay.

And drinking was easier than food. Easier than hiding the rituals of bulimia. Alcohol didn't feel shameful. It didn't demand secrecy or leave me trembling on a bathroom floor. It felt like permission – to soften, to let go, to not feel so much.

I didn't make a clean break from bulimia. The two overlapped for quite a while. I'd purge in the afternoon, drink at night. Binge and blackout. It was like playing tug-of-war between two demons and letting them both win. I bounced from one form of chaos to the next, searching for calm and never quite finding it.

Eventually, bulimia faded – not because I healed, but because drinking was quieter. Easier to hide. Easier to explain. It felt like a deal with the devil – only instead of flames and pitchforks, he came with a red Solo cup and a crooked smile. *Here, try this instead*, he said. And I did.

And for a while, it worked. On the surface, I kept up the act. I still got good grades, played sports, smiled in pictures. I showed up. From the outside, I looked like just another teenager blowing off steam. Drinking didn't look like addiction – it looked like fitting in.

But I wasn't drinking to party. I was drinking to survive.

Even so, not everyone was fooled. My sister didn't know the full extent, but she noticed things – how I came home wired or out of it, how my energy shifted. She'd give me a look and say, "Vaness, take it easy," with that mix of love and concern only a big sister can deliver. I'd laugh it off, roll my eyes, act like she was overreacting. But deep down, I knew she saw through it – and that made it harder to lie to myself. Still, I wanted the buzzing to stop – and alcohol promised a softer kind of quiet.

Alcohol became my silence. My escape hatch. Where bulimia had been a scream for control, drinking became a lullaby – soft, seductive. It blurred the edges until I almost believed I was okay.

Almost.

Chapter Five

Damage, Rearranged

The captivating melody of alcohol followed me into college – seductive, familiar, and just loud enough to drown out everything else. I went to UMass Amherst, where drinking didn't just fit in – it thrived. Nicknamed "ZooMass" for a reason, the campus pulsed with chaos, and I was living in Southwest – the heart of the party scene. Recklessness was rewarded. Hangovers were punchlines. Blackouts were bragging rights. Everyone drank too much, so no one noticed when someone crossed a line.

And I crossed the line. Again and again.

There were nights I couldn't remember. Mornings I couldn't piece together. I laughed about it, like everyone else did. But beneath the laughter was a truth I couldn't shake: I wasn't drinking for fun. I was drinking for relief.

Still, I kept it together – or at least, that's how it looked. I made it to most of my classes, juggled part-time jobs, and did what I needed to do to keep up appearances. I finished college with good grades. I showed up. I smiled. On the outside, I looked like I was doing just fine. But beneath it all, I was quietly coming undone. I was learning how to succeed and self-destruct at the same time.

And it didn't stop after graduation. Alcohol came with me into adulthood – into my first job, my early twenties, my version of "real life." My heels clicked confidently across office floors while hangovers clung to me like a second skin. I answered emails, met deadlines, smiled through morning meetings with a churning stomach and bloodshot eyes. Listerine masked the stale scent of alcohol on my breath. I looked the part.

But I was still just a girl searching for an off switch. I had mastered the mask – polished on the outside, fraying underneath. The scariest part wasn't that I was falling apart. It was that I had normalized it.

I knew it was too much – the way one glass always led to another, and then another, until stopping didn't even feel like an option. It was like a faucet turned all the way on – once it started, I couldn't shut it off. A quiet voice inside me asked questions I didn't want to answer. So I pushed it down. I told myself I was functioning. I had a job. I paid my bills. I showed up for people.

It's not like I was drinking from a paper bag on a street corner.

Or like my grandfather.

He was the only biological grandparent I ever met – my only living one – and I don't have many memories of him. Just one, really. He was in a hospital bed, his belly swollen with cirrhosis from heavy drinking, the room thick with silence and something I didn't yet have words for. I was too young to understand what was happening, but old enough to feel the grief heavy in the air like smoke. My family stood around him, whispering goodbyes while I lingered at the edge of the bed, confused and quiet.

Years later, I understood. And still, I told myself I was different. What took him couldn't possibly take me. I had it under control. Or so I thought. *That* was what I believed alcoholism looked like – obvious, tragic, unmistakable. I didn't see myself in that picture.

So I told myself I was fine.

Not even the night I woke up in a hospital bed after blacking out could convince me otherwise. I had been out with coworkers, celebrating another long day. I still don't know exactly what happened – only that I was found slumped against a building outside the bar, left like a forgotten coat. Someone must have called an ambulance, but I never found out who. One minute I was laughing over drinks, the next I was in a hospital bed, trying to piece together the night like a movie with entire scenes missing.

A close friend from work picked me up from the ER the next morning, my hospital bracelet still wrapped around my wrist. She didn't grill me with questions or pass judgment – just drove us to get coffee, then straight to the office. I told myself it was just another night with too much. No big deal. That was the lie I clung to – because admitting otherwise was too terrifying.

I could still laugh. Still function. Still check the boxes. I didn't realize that high-functioning is still struggling. That smiling is not the same as healing. And that the most dangerous kind of drinking isn't always loud or messy – sometimes, it's quiet. Polished. Hidden in plain sight.

But the truth was harder to face.

No one tells you that alcohol doesn't erase pain – it just presses pause. And when the buzz fades, the pain returns. Louder. Sharper. Angrier. Every unprocessed feeling. Every wound. Every ache. So I drank again. And again. Until I couldn't tell if I was drinking because I wanted to or because I didn't know how not to.

This wasn't rebellion. It wasn't fun. It was survival. I had traded one form of self-destruction for another. Handed off bulimia like a bruised offering, hoping alcohol could carry the weight. But I hadn't healed. I had only rearranged the damage.

I was still trying to feel okay. Still trying to disappear. Still trying not to feel anything at all.

Chapter Six

The Beautiful Mess

And then, I met someone who made me feel again. Not panic. Not shame. Joy.

I met him at work.

At first, it was all flirty banter and group happy hours – the kind of lightness that made everything else – stress, anxiety, the quiet ache of not knowing who I really was – fade into the background. We were both still carrying the weight of rocky relationships, not quite over them but just far enough past the breaking points to pretend that we were. A little bruised, a little guarded. But Matt made me laugh. Really laugh. The kind that lets the light in through places you thought were sealed shut.

But it wasn't just the laughter. Matt didn't wear a mask – not the way I had for most of my life. There was no filter. He said what he thought, even when it came out blunt or occasionally a little insulting. And surprisingly, I found that refreshing. Even comforting. After years of tiptoeing around other people's feelings and hiding parts of myself to keep the peace, there was something grounding about someone who just... said it. Who didn't try to sugarcoat everything. It felt honest. Disarming. Real.

It all moved fast. Passionate. Messy and fun. There were city nights at sporting events, weekends filled with bar tabs and live music, parties that blurred into morning coffee runs.

We weren't rushing out of recklessness – it just felt like we both knew. We were ready for something different. Something real. And we found it in each other.

It wasn't perfect. The beginning had its bumps – moments of jealousy, miscommunication, and the usual growing pains that come when two independent people try to merge their already full lives. But underneath it all, there was a steady pull toward each other. We just fit. And somewhere along the way, without even realizing it, we both loosened our grip on the relationships we had still been half-holding onto. The past no longer had a place in what we were beginning to build.

Looking back, I can understand why I had clung so tightly to old relationships – even ones that hurt me. Letting go never came easily to me. I always stayed too long, tried too hard, convinced that if I could just hold on tighter, I could fix it – fix me. I hadn't yet learned that love shouldn't require you to shrink yourself. That I didn't have to disappear in order to be loved.

But with Matt, something softened. I didn't have to perform or prove anything. I could just be – and for the first time, that was enough. We both knew, not long after, that we didn't want to do life without each other.

Marriage and starting a family came quickly – fast, full of love, and a little chaotic.

You might think giving up drinking during pregnancy would've been a huge challenge – but surprisingly, it wasn't. Not for me. It wasn't easy, exactly, but it also wasn't some dramatic fight or rock-bottom moment. For the first time, I had something greater than the urge to numb. I had purpose. Focus. Control – but not the damaging kind. The kind that grows life, not erases it.

I was growing a human. And that stunned me. Humbled me.

There were complications early on – pain that intensified quickly, and sciatica that made even walking and driving difficult. I'd always been used to my body struggling more than most, but this felt different. Like something deeper was being stirred awake. I ended up leaving my job, and just like that, my entire world narrowed down to one mission: protect this tiny, incredible being growing inside of me. It was terrifying. And beautiful. And for the first time, all-consuming in a way that didn't destroy me – it anchored me.

I devoured *What to Expect When You're Expecting,* obsessing over every little detail – what size she was each week, what parts of her were forming, what I could do to help her grow. I'd call my sister constantly, comparing symptoms and asking questions – she had been through it all already with my niece and nephew. I had loved them like they were my own, and now, holding this new life inside me, it felt like I was stepping into something I had quietly prepared for all along. Every symptom, every flutter, every milestone became a thread pulling me closer to her.

It was still obsession – but it felt different than the kind I'd known before. It wasn't rooted in fear or control or self-destruction. Not like food. Not like alcohol. This was the kind of fixation that came from love. From awe. From the overwhelming responsibility and privilege of carrying a life. And for once, my hyper-focus wasn't about shrinking or escaping. It was about showing up – fully – for someone else.

Becoming a mother was the most magical thing I'd ever experienced – nothing had ever felt so right, so immediate, so pure. But alongside the magic came a deeper undercurrent of fear. A new kind. Subtle, but steady. I wasn't just looking out for myself anymore – I was caring for someone completely dependent on me.

The weight of that responsibility settled in gently but firmly, shifting something inside me.

With all that unfolding, you'd think what came next would have knocked me off balance. Our firstborn was only three months old when we found out I was pregnant again. There was no planning – just a sudden wave of disbelief, followed by surrender. And yet, it didn't rattle me. I welcomed it. Even with the exhaustion and the unknowns, pregnancy felt sacred. There was a quiet power in it – a softness and strength that coexisted inside me.

My body, which I had spent so many years fighting, finally felt trustworthy. Purposeful. I was building something real, something lasting, something full of life. And for the first time, I felt full of life, too. There was peace in it. A deep, steady knowing that I was exactly where I was meant to be. I was ready to do it all again – to grow another life, shaped by everything I had learned the first time around.

And so we did. Before long, one child became two, then three – three babies in under three years. Our days were filled with diapers and bottles, sleepy snuggles and toddler chaos. They tumbled over each other like a living, breathing pile of joy and exhaustion.

Each child brought their own magic. Madilyn carried the calm wisdom of an old soul. Olivia, the soft glow of light and sweetness. And our baby boy, Cameron, was pure spark and mischief. We built a beautiful mess. A home full of love – and noise.

And yet, somehow, we still kept the party going. Regular weekend get-togethers with friends. Drinks flowing while toddlers slept upstairs or crawled underfoot. Laughter echoing through the house, music thumping from Bluetooth speakers, bottles clinking on the counters. I played the role well – hostess, mom, wife, the one who "had it all together." Three kids in tow, diaper bags packed, snacks prepped, birthday gifts bought, wine always in hand. Always.

It was so much. So loud. So constant. But once again – I got it done. Because that's what I did. Even when I was tired to the bone. Even when I felt myself fraying at the edges. Even when I knew, deep down, that the wine wasn't just a way to unwind – it was becoming a way to cope. Again. But I couldn't face that. Not yet.

Because everything looked good from the outside. Because love was real. Because our life was full. Because I still didn't know how to ask for help. So I smiled, poured another drink, and kept showing up. And still, somehow, I held it all together.

And then – just as I was beginning to feel the weight of everything I'd been holding up – grief came knocking. Loud, sudden, and impossible to ignore.

Chapter Seven

The Space He Left

It started with a headache.

But the story – the real story – began long before that.

My relationship with my father had always been complicated. Not in the way that burns bridges or ends with slammed doors, but in the way that leaves you reaching – always reaching – for something just a little out of grasp.

I was so young when my parents divorced. Too young to understand what was happening, but old enough to feel the ache of absence. When my mother moved my sister and me from New Hampshire to Florida, everything shifted. Suddenly, we lived in two different worlds – two different climates, two different homes, two different lives. Over the years, both of my parents remarried, and the landscape of our family kept changing. There were step-parents. Step-siblings. Rotating holidays and packed summer visits. Birthdays missed or celebrated late. Compromises made. Emotions tucked away. We made it work. But it never felt seamless. Never easy.

VANESSA FRANCE

And still – he was my dad.

Big laugh. Big hugs. Big presence. He had this booming voice that filled a room, a bear hug that made everything else fall away for a moment. He loved hard, told great stories, and drank more than he should. But when he laughed – really laughed – it stirred something deep inside you. You couldn't help but join in.

As I grew older, things got a little easier between us. We all eventually made our way back to New England, and with proximity came more chances. More shared moments. More opportunities to try again. We were still learning each other in pieces – never quite whole, but reaching. Always reaching.

And then, just as he was about to finally settle into the life he'd long dreamed of – everything changed. He had just retired. Almost sixty years old. Ready to move to Arizona with his new wife and chase the desert sun. He was done working, done rushing. He was going to breathe for the first time in decades. This was supposed to be his chapter. Finally.

But the headaches came.

At first, he brushed them off. So did his doctor. Maybe stress. Maybe tension headaches. But they didn't stop. They got sharper. More frequent. The headaches became relentless. He started to lose balance. He veered off the road while driving. Something wasn't right.

And then came the word I had never heard before: Glioblastoma.

Brain cancer. Fast. Aggressive. Incurable.

They gave him two choices. Do nothing, and he might have three months. Fight with surgery, radiation, and chemo, and he might have eighteen.

He chose to fight.

And God, was that hard. Watching someone with such a huge spirit – this larger-than-life presence – slowly diminish. Watching the light in his eyes dim beneath hospital fluorescents. Watching him change. Lose balance. Struggle to finish a thought. Watching the man I knew disappear, one fragile piece at a time.

Our relationship had never been tidy. It was never wrapped up in clean conversations or picture-perfect moments. It was jagged and real and stitched together with love and regret. But in those final weeks – when the world shrank to a hospice room – the sharpness softened. There was quiet. There was stillness. There was something sacred. We didn't say much. We didn't have to. There was a shared knowing that passed between us – wordless, weightless, heavy all the same.

I held his hand. He squeezed mine. And that was enough.

My sister and I were beside him when he took his last breath. My children were there, too – so young, so quiet. Around the bed stood the people who had loved him across seasons – exes and in-laws, old friends and family, by blood and by bond – and none of the labels mattered in that room. Love wasn't keeping score. Barbara, his wife, cared for him with a steady, unshowy devotion that humbled me. Van Morrison played softly in the background, his voice drifting through the room like a prayer. It felt suspended in time. Gentle. As if the music itself was helping him let go. It was a holy kind of moment – heartbreaking and beautiful all at once.

Watching a parent leave this world changes you. Permanently. Quietly. From the inside out. It shifts your center of gravity. It cracks you open in places you didn't know were closed. It makes you question what you inherited. What you're still carrying. What you wish you'd let go of sooner. It teaches you that love doesn't always come neatly packaged. That sometimes it shows up clumsy. Late. Wounded. But it's still love.

And that's what we had. Complicated. Incomplete. But real. And in the middle of all those tangled feelings, something quietly shifted inside me – something I didn't yet have words for. It stirred open like a door I hadn't noticed before, nudged by the weight of what I had witnessed. The stillness. The music. The way presence alone could become a kind of offering. I didn't know it then, but something in me had begun to turn toward that threshold – toward the divine space between life and death.

Now, there's a space my dad used to fill – loudly, joyfully, unmistakably – that echoes in the most unexpected places. In my laugh. In the way I throw my arms around my own kids. He's in the parts of me that still reach for one more bear hug, one more joke, one more moment to look him in the eye and say: *I know you tried. I did too. And I love you for it.*

And life, in its strange and steady way, continued on. Grief left its mark – quiet and permanent – but so did something else. Love. Legacy.

And the realization that sometimes, just when one chapter closes, another arrives in the most unexpected form.

Chapter Eight

When Jack Arrived

Which is how, just when we thought we were done – when the strollers were folded away, the diapers finally behind us, and the house beginning to feel like it might just settle into a rhythm – God placed one more unexpected gift in our hands.

Another baby. Another boy. Another chapter we never saw coming.

This beautiful boy was our surprise. But from the moment he arrived, it felt like he'd been part of the plan all along.

I'll never forget the moment at the doctor's office when they told me his due date: my dad's birthday. I just stared at them, stunned. Of all the dates. It felt like more than coincidence – like some invisible thread pulling us all together.

We named him Jack – a nod to my father, John. It felt right. Strong, simple, full of love.

I often imagine how much my dad would have adored him – scooping him up in those big bear arms, laughing loud and proud, calling him "my little buddy." I like to believe he knew Jack was coming. That maybe, in some unseen way, they passed each other – one soul leaving, and another arriving.

Jack didn't just bring new life into our family – he shifted the way we moved through it. This sweet baby boy was quiet, observant, and full of a soft kind of magic. He'd flap his little arms like a sweet baby bird ready to take flight – pure joy pulsing through his tiny body. He would sit, mesmerized, watching the wheels of his toy train spin as he pushed it back and forth. Over and over. While the other kids bounced from room to room, Jack stayed in his own little world – content, peaceful, and perfectly in sync with himself.

At the age when most toddlers start engaging in pretend play and stringing together little phrases, Jack moved differently through the world. He didn't seek out the usual back-and-forth games or mimic the chatter of his siblings. But he was smart – so smart. And with three older siblings constantly orbiting around him, I chalked it up to the chaos. They talked for him, answered for him, brought him what he needed before he ever had to ask. Maybe he was just going with the flow. But I have to admit, something in me wondered.

At his 18-month well visit, everything shifted.

"How many words does he have?" the pediatrician asked, watching him bounce and flap a little anxiously on the exam table.

"Maybe a couple?" I answered hesitantly. "Mama. Dada. Not much more."

Her tone changed. She gently suggested a referral – to rule things out, to learn more. And many months later, right around when he turned two years old, after evaluations and observations and a string of appointments I don't fully remember now, Jack was diagnosed with Autism Spectrum Disorder.

I cried in the car afterward. Not because I was scared of who Jack was – I already knew his heart, his light, the quiet brilliance he carried. But because, in that moment, I felt the ground shift beneath me. I gripped the steering wheel and let the tears fall – hot, quiet, relentless – not from fear of him, but from fear of not being enough for him. Of getting it wrong. Of not being able to give him what he needed in a world that didn't always feel built for softness, for difference, for the kind of magic that didn't fit into tidy checkboxes.

I sat there, parked outside the doctor's office with the hum of the engine in my ears and the weight of the diagnosis settling into my chest like a fog I couldn't see through. What would life look like now? What would he struggle with? Would he be okay? Would we?

There was a kind of mourning in that moment – not for Jack, but for the version of the future I had quietly, unknowingly imagined. And as that version dissolved, what remained was uncertainty – wide and uncharted. But underneath it, quietly and firmly, was love. The kind that says: no matter what, we will figure this out. Together.

As we began to wrap our minds around the diagnosis, we also began to step more fully into Jack's world. And that meant learning what autism really was – not a single story, not a checklist, but a spectrum. No two people experience it the same way. At first, we didn't see "signs." We just saw Jack – unique, particular, sometimes tricky to soothe. We thought he simply didn't like baths. That he just really loved letters. That the meltdowns were tantrums, or that he was just especially sensitive or stubborn. But slowly, the diagnosis helped us understand there was more going on beneath the surface.

Many children on the spectrum process the world through a sensory lens that most of us never even think about. Things that seem "normal" to our senses – background noise, bright lights, the texture of clothing – can feel overwhelming, even painful.

For Jack, the world came in loud, bright, and fast. Noise flooded his nervous system. The rustling of a plastic bag, the slice of a knife cutting into an apple – even the simplest sounds could completely derail him. So he would stim – a self-soothing technique used by many on the spectrum to regulate and cope. Jack would jump up and down, flap his arms, sometimes cover his ears. This was how he calmed himself when everything became too much. How he created a sense of safety in a world that often felt too loud, too fast, too much.

Baths were another challenge. The feeling of water on his skin could send him into full distress. What should've been a simple routine became a layered process of patience, creativity, and listening in new ways. We had to adjust our pace, our expectations, and our definitions of progress. We had to meet him where he was.

The meltdowns were intense. Sometimes he'd hold his breath until his face turned red. Other times, in a swirl of frustration and helplessness, he'd hit his head against the floor or wall – not out of defiance, but desperation. Jack knew what he wanted; he just didn't have the words yet to tell us. That gap between what he understood and what he could express built into a frustration he didn't know how to release – and all we could do was stay with him, gently, and ride it out until it passed.

And in that space – in the stillness of his own rhythm – there was wonder. Jack learned the alphabet with lightning speed. By the time he was three, he had moved on to the Russian alphabet. He would watch a video once, memorize the letters, recite them back, and write them. He carried his bath alphabet with him everywhere, repeating his favorite letters – "R" and "H" – like cherished friends. His mind moved differently. Quickly. Creatively. Mysteriously. It was mesmerizing to witness.

And while we were learning to see and understand his world, we were never doing it alone. We didn't have a roadmap, but we had each other – and almost immediately after his diagnosis, our support system wrapped around us.

We were incredibly lucky – and I don't say that lightly. We live just steps away from my in-laws, and their presence made all the difference. Mimi, Jack's grandmother, had spent her career in schools and special education, and she stepped in immediately with ideas and encouragement. She helped build crash pads, create sensory-friendly activities, and guided us with the kind of steady wisdom that only comes from lived experience and love.

And it wasn't just her. Our entire family – Jack's uncles and aunts, my own mom, my sister, stepdad, and extended relatives on both sides – showed up in ways that still bring tears to my eyes.

My sister in particular had a way of being steady without needing to fix anything. She didn't pretend to have all the answers – she just listened. She sat with me through the confusion and grief, sometimes holding space in silence, sometimes gently helping me find words for what felt impossible to name. Even when we were both overwhelmed, she made sure I knew I wasn't alone. That kind of support – the kind that doesn't try to solve, just stays – was everything.

There was so much love around us – not just spoken, but lived. And in a season that could have easily felt overwhelming, we were reminded again and again: we weren't doing this alone. We were held. Surrounded. Blessed.

Our home became part sanctuary, part therapy center – walls lined with visual schedules, crash pads softening the corners, therapists cross-legged on the floor guiding Jack through the slow, deliberate work of connection. They became our everyday angels – patient, practical, relentless in their kindness – showing up week after week. Some days we welcomed them into our living room; other days we dropped him off at centers where he was just one of many little ones trying to find their way. Every new tool tugged at my heart – a reminder of both the challenges and the fierce love reshaping our days.

And still, most nights ended the same. After the therapists left, and the dishes were done, and the last bedtime book was read, I'd pour my wine. It dulled the edges of worry, softened the ache of missing my dad, numbed the quiet fear that I wasn't enough. I told myself it was deserved. But really, it was dependence in disguise.

But Jack – Jack pulled me back to the present, again and again. His joy was undiluted. His presence, pure. He didn't ask me to be perfect. He asked me to see him. And in doing that, I began to see myself again – beneath the fear, beyond the grief. One glance, one moment, one small step at a time, he was teaching me how to stay. How to be here. Not numbing. Not escaping. Just breathing into the life we were building – hard, holy, real.

Chapter Nine

The Gift of Returning

Just as we were nearing the end of another long stretch of therapy appointments and uncertainty, a new door opened: an invitation to Jack's in-person evaluation at a full-time special education program in the next town over. I didn't know what to expect – only that this would determine whether he qualified, and if this school might be the right fit.

The evaluation was one of the hardest we'd been through. At one point, Jack's beloved alphabet letters were taken away as part of the assessment, and he lost it – the kind of full-body meltdown we had come to know too well, the kind I could feel building before it broke. His body tensed, his cries sharp and desperate – the heartbreak of a little boy who knew what he needed but didn't yet have the words to express it.

I had been instructed to stay behind the line of desks. Not to intervene. Not to comfort. Just to observe. But everything in me rebelled. My hands clenched the edge of the chair. My heart raced. Every fiber of my being wanted to rush to him – to wrap him in my arms, to protect him from this unfamiliar room, these unfamiliar faces, this ache he didn't know how to name.

And then I saw her. The lead teacher. She moved toward him with a calm that felt warm and instinctive. She didn't flinch at the flailing or the tears. She didn't scold or restrain. Instead, she knelt beside him, guiding him gently toward the crash pad with a steadiness that grounded the moment. Her presence didn't seek control – it offered comfort. Understanding. Safety.

I watched through tear-filled eyes, the weight of powerlessness giving way to something else – awe, relief, a deep and aching gratitude. She saw him – really saw him – even in his most dysregulated state. And in that moment, something inside me softened. I knew, without question, she was meant for him. That he would be understood. That he would be safe.

What made the outcome of the evaluation even more emotional was learning that, if accepted, Jack would spend his days in a completely sub-separate classroom – a quiet space designed entirely for his needs, with no big crowds, no overstimulation, and no pressure to keep up. He would work one-on-one with a dedicated team – and at the heart of that team was the very same lead teacher who had seen him so clearly during the evaluation. It felt like both a relief and a moment of clarity – a recognition that he needed something different, and a deep gratitude that it even existed.

When Jack was officially accepted into the program, it marked a quiet but powerful shift – a mix of fear, hope, and bittersweet relief. The house grew quieter. The days stretched a little longer. And for the first time, all four of our children were in school.

Letting go was still hard. But it didn't feel like abandonment – it felt like trust. And in the quiet that followed – the slower mornings, the longer stretches of time – I began to feel something else rise to the surface. Suddenly, there was space. Possibility. A bit of breathing room I hadn't realized I was craving. And with that space came an old, familiar tug – the desire to return to work. To use my voice again. To remember who I was beyond nap schedules and therapy appointments.

I told myself maybe this was it – the season that would finally make everything feel steadier. Maybe if I could just find something meaningful to pour myself into, I wouldn't need wine at the end of every day to soften the edges. I was still searching for something to hold onto – something real enough to keep me grounded.

Even as Jack was finding his place in the world, I kept thinking back to another space I had stood in not long before – one that had reshaped me in ways I was only beginning to understand. Sitting with my dad in hospice – holding his hand, breathing with him as he slipped from this world to the next – left a mark on me that would never fully fade. What I witnessed wasn't just death. It was love, stripped down to its most essential form. It was presence. It was peace.

Hospice didn't fix the pain – but it held it. Gently. Without force. Without fear. And somewhere in that stillness, something inside me had shifted. A seed was planted.

My sister felt it, too. She had stood beside me in that same space – shoulder to shoulder, heart to heart. And not long after my father passed, she made a bold and beautiful decision: she left behind her 25-year career as a hairstylist and enrolled in nursing school. She wanted to become a hospice nurse. It was one of the bravest things I've ever witnessed – a complete pivot into purpose. I was, and still am, so deeply proud of her.

Her courage sparked something in me. While I didn't see myself becoming a nurse, I realized there was still a place for me in that world – a way to serve, to connect, to offer presence and clarity during life's most tender moments. With my background in communication and sales, I stepped into the role of hospice liaison – a bridge between the medical world and the families navigating it. I could be a calm voice. A steady hand. Someone who met people in their fear and offered something grounding. Human. Real.

It wasn't just Jack's new school schedule that allowed me to re-enter the working world – it was my father's passing that gave me direction. That gave me a reason. I didn't want a job. I wanted to do something that mattered. I wanted to step more fully into the spaces I had already come to know so intimately – the threshold between life and death. Because once you've seen what hospice truly is, you don't forget. You carry it with you. And if you're lucky, you find a way to give it back.

I loved the work – and the incredible team I was honored to join. I built relationships quickly and dove headfirst into the job, pouring my soul into it. I wasn't just explaining logistics – I was helping people understand what hospice truly was: a gift. A sacred opportunity to bring comfort, presence, and peace to life's final chapter. For a couple of years, I gave everything I had to that role – educating, guiding, and holding space with my whole heart.

Even though it was a lot – juggling a full-time job, four kids with their own sports and therapy schedules, and a husband who sometimes traveled for work – I was doing it. I was stretched thin, yes, but I felt aligned. Purposeful. Like I had found something that fit.

What I didn't know yet – what none of us could have known – was that the world as we knew it was about to change. Drastically.

Chapter Ten

When The World Fell Apart

The cracks split wide open in 2020. When the world shut down, so did I.

For someone who already lived with anxiety – the kind that scans every room for exits, rehearses tragedies before they happen, and braces for disaster even in moments of calm – a global pandemic wasn't just frightening. It was proof. Proof that the worst-case scenarios I'd always imagined weren't irrational after all. That fear could be justified. It was like someone had turned the volume all the way up on every quiet dread I'd ever carried.

And because I was working in hospice, I didn't just read about the death tolls – I felt them. I heard them in phone calls from overwhelmed nurses, in sobbing family members who couldn't say goodbye, in the steady stream of names listed off during our team calls. COVID didn't just make death a statistic – it made it constant. The unthinkable wasn't just possible – it was happening. And my nervous system, already worn from years of hypervigilance, finally had confirmation of what it had always feared: the rug can be pulled, and everything can fall.

As the world changed, so did my work. Much of our role as hospice liaisons took place inside nursing homes and hospitals – building trust with staff, connecting with families, and helping patients transition into end-of-life care. But when COVID swept in, everything familiar fell apart.

The job I had grown to love – sharing the gift of hospice, helping to guide patients and their families through some of the most intimate, heartbreaking, and beautiful moments of life – suddenly became something unrecognizable.

Before the pandemic, there had been peace in that work. A sense of purpose. Holding hands, offering comfort, watching families gather to surround their loved one with warmth and presence at the end of their journey. It was tender, holy work.

But overnight, that sacred offering was taken from us. The soft rituals of goodbye were replaced with protocols and distance. Families were told they couldn't be in the room. Couldn't hold a hand. Couldn't say "I love you" into the ear of someone slipping away. Instead, they were forced to watch from behind screens – an iPad propped up by trembling hands, a fragile window into a goodbye that was never meant to be witnessed from afar.

Day after day, I sat with it – the sorrow, the injustice, the helplessness. I carried the weight of stories I couldn't share, of losses I couldn't ease, of goodbyes that were never given the dignity they deserved. What was once meaningful had become devastating. And there was no time to process it. No space to breathe. Just more heartbreak. More screens. More silence where connection used to be.

And somehow, despite it all, my bosses acted like nothing had changed. Meetings, albeit virtual, went on as usual. Numbers were everything. We were still expected to "share the gift of hospice" – while being measured by metrics and quotas, as if this sacred work could be boiled down to a spreadsheet.

It was cold. It was inhumane. And it killed me inside.

I was grieving things I couldn't name, barely staying afloat – and they put me on a performance plan. As if I were failing. Lazy. Unmotivated. As if the problem wasn't the unbearable weight of carrying others' pain while barely surviving my own. As if we hadn't been locked out of the very spaces where our work was meant to happen – the nursing homes, hospitals, and care facilities that had sealed their doors, cutting us off from the presence and connection our job depended on.

I understood the pressure was trickling down – everyone answering to forces above them – and still, from where I sat, it felt like a cruel joke.

Here I was – quietly dying inside – while being told to perform empathy. To smile. To inspire trust. To sell peace while choking on my own pain. I clung to survival in whatever ways I could – including the coworker who answered every one of my desperate phone calls, her steady voice a reminder that I wasn't completely alone in it. I kept showing up because I didn't know how not to. Because I was still trying to be the girl who got it all right. Because the performance was the only thing I had left.

The scary part wasn't that I was falling apart. It was that I had normalized it. But the cost of holding it all would eventually come due. Meanwhile, at home, chaos reigned.

All four of our children were suddenly learning from laptops, scattered across bedrooms and kitchen tables, trying to make sense of a world that no longer made any. I was juggling work, while my own family – my husband, my kids – were slowly breaking down too. And I couldn't hold it all.

And then there was Jack. Our kindergartner. Brilliant, sensitive, autistic – and forced to sit on a screen and pretend it was school. He didn't need help learning letters or numbers – he knew the answers before the teachers even asked. What he needed was connection. Peers. Social cues. Time with other children. And that was the very thing taken from him. Instead of giving him the support he truly needed, his world was reduced to a glitchy screen and muted squares.

He sat through it in tears and confusion, not understanding why he had to stare at a screen while no one really saw him. It was awful to make him endure something so misaligned with who he was, what he needed. He deserved so much more – and I couldn't give it to him. Not then. Not in that moment.

Because that same kitchen table – where he sat crying, overwhelmed, and lost – was the same table I used as my hospice office. I would be juggling trying to assist him, coax him through the lesson, while also on the phone with a hospital social worker or a nurse at the care facility, organizing end-of-life plans for a new patient coming onto our hospice services. I was coordinating death while my son desperately needed help with kindergarten. I was split in half – trying to be present for two worlds that were both slipping through my fingers.

So I drank. I drank to quiet the panic that never really left my chest. I drank to dull the guilt of watching all four of my children struggle in ways I couldn't fix – their young, growing minds forced to absorb a world laced with fear, isolation, and confusion. I drank to silence the ache of seeing their spark dim, their bodies restless from too much screen time and too little connection. I drank to push down the helplessness of not being able to give them what they needed – and the shame of knowing I wasn't giving myself what I needed either. I drank to blur the sharp edges of the day: the death notifications, the zoom meltdowns, the eerie quiet of a house that once felt full of life. I drank to survive the masks we all wore – not just on our faces, but in our lives.

And it got worse. So much worse. It wasn't casual anymore. It wasn't just a couple glasses. It was every single night. Without fail. A bottle, usually more. Eventually, I lost count altogether – we had started buying the big black boxes of wine, the kind that held the equivalent of four bottles. One box would disappear faster than I ever admitted out loud.

Wine became my buffer. My breath at the end of a day when I hadn't taken any real ones. It was my reward, my numbing agent, my quiet agreement with myself that I'd made it through another impossible stretch. It didn't matter that the pain was still there when the box was empty. It didn't matter that the chaos didn't stop. For a few short hours, I could pretend the lines weren't so blurred – between work and home, between grief and guilt, between surviving and actually living.

I told myself I was hiding it well. That no one could see the cracks. That if I smiled enough, worked hard enough, poured just the right amount into my glass, I could keep it all from falling apart.

But children always see.

Especially my sweet Olivia. Lali, as we call her, is my youngest daughter – nine years old at the time – the one who has always been so much like me, for better or worse. Sensitive. Intuitive. Constantly observing the world with eyes that see far more than most people realize. She feels things deeply, carries things quietly, and has inherited some of the same anxious wiring I've struggled with my whole life. She holds it all in silence – until it leaks out in questions and worry and tears that come from somewhere too deep to name.

She had been watching me for a while – not judging, not accusing, just quietly absorbing.

And then came the night I'll never forget.

VANESSA FRANCE

It was one of those strange, disorienting pandemic days – where time felt stuck, the world was sideways, and nothing felt certain or safe. I was sitting in my usual spot on the couch, wine glass in hand, when she started heading up to bed – her little shoulders heavy from a world she didn't yet have the words to explain. Masks, rules, distance. It was all so much. She reached the bottom of the stairs and paused. And then she turned.

She didn't speak. She just looked at me. Really looked. Her eyes met mine – not in a casual way, but with a kind of knowing that sent a chill through me. She searched my face, then, as if pulled by gravity, let her gaze drop slowly to the wine glass in my hand. It wasn't a glance – it was deliberate, heavy, lingering. Her eyes stayed there, still and silent, before rising back up to meet mine again. It was only a few short seconds, but it felt like a lifetime.

And in that look – that quiet, gutting, too-wise-for-her-age look – everything passed between us. The confusion. The sadness. The unspoken question: *Why do you need that, Mama?*

She didn't ask it aloud. She didn't have to. It was in her eyes. Her expression. The way she stood there – tiny and strong and heartbroken all at once. And something in me shattered. Because I knew that look. I had worn that look as a little girl, trying to understand the grown-ups around me, trying to make sense of their pain. And now I was the one putting it in her eyes. I was the source. And I hated that.

I hated that my anxiety had become her worry and my coping her concern – that this version of me was what she was absorbing. In that moment, something in me broke. It was a reckoning – the beginning of the long walk from breakdown to breakthrough. A clear, piercing realization: the pain I was trying to numb was touching the people I loved most.

And once I saw it, I couldn't unsee it. Something shifted after that night – subtle but irreversible. Like a door had opened in my mind, and even though I wasn't ready to walk through it just yet, I could feel the air changing. The truth was rising. I couldn't outrun it anymore. I couldn't pretend it wasn't costing me something real.

And then one morning soon after – I'll never forget it – I woke up so hungover I could barely lift my head. My mouth was dry, my heart pounding, the room spinning just enough to make me question everything. But in the middle of that familiar misery, the fog that had dulled everything for so long lifted just enough for the truth to land.

If I don't stop, I might not wake up next time.

The thought struck like lightning. Sharp. Final. True. It was as clear as anything I'd ever known. In one heartbreaking instant, I saw the full weight of what was at stake: my children growing up motherless. My husband mourning the woman he once knew. The life I had fought so hard to build – messy, beautiful, chaotic, and full – gone because I couldn't let go of the thing that was slowly killing me. I saw it all. And I couldn't look away.

That was the day everything changed. November 9th, 2020. The day I chose to live. The day I said goodbye to the one thing I thought I couldn't live without – so that I could finally start living. Fully. Honestly. Present.

It wasn't the end of the story. It was the beginning of the most brutal chapter yet. But it was also the first real step home.

Chapter Eleven

The Climb

Coming home to yourself sounds beautiful – full of healing, warmth, and hope. But after years of disconnection, it wasn't soft. It wasn't easy. It felt more like fumbling through a thick fog – one uncertain step at a time, with no clear path forward.

Because the truth is, deciding to stop drinking was only the beginning – a quiet, solitary choice no one else could see. What followed was a slow surfacing of all I had pushed down. I was raw, restless, wide awake – stripped of the numbness that used to shield me, unsure of who I was without it.

What surprised me most was how quickly my system panicked without it.

Withdrawal came first – subtle at times, then sharp and jarring. My body, used to wine lulling it to sleep night after night, no longer knew how to shut down on its own. I was wired and exhausted all at once, pacing the floors while my family slept, heart pounding in my chest like a warning. My hands trembled. My brain raced. There were nights I would stare at the ceiling for hours, willing the silence to quiet the chaos inside me. But it didn't.

I felt like I had left my body entirely – like I was watching a stranger move through the motions of my life. Feed the kids. Do the laundry. Pick up the house. Keep it together. Outwardly, everything looked the same. But inside, everything had shifted. Only my husband knew I had stopped drinking. I didn't tell anyone else at first – not because I wasn't serious, but because I was scared. Scared it wouldn't last. Scared I'd fail. So I carried it alone, unsure if this new path would hold.

We were in the heart of the pandemic, and in many ways, we were all already hidden – quarantined from each other, from the world, from ourselves. Our lives had shrunk to the size of our living room. Our kitchen table was now a classroom. The backyard was the only escape. There were no playdates, no visitors, no one dropping by unannounced. And so I came undone quietly, privately – slipping apart in the background where no one could see.

And around that same time, I had made a difficult but necessary decision – I left my job. Hospice had once felt like a calling, sacred work that honored life's most fragile moments. But during COVID, everything changed. The emotional toll was relentless. The grief was constant. And the pressure from my bosses became simply unbearable – unrealistic expectations, no room to breathe, and no acknowledgment of what we were carrying.

Still, letting go wasn't easy. I had always been a people pleaser. Quitting wasn't in me. I didn't want to disappoint anyone, didn't want to look like I had failed. But deep down, I knew I couldn't keep pouring from an empty cup. I couldn't hold space for death and dying while trying to claw my way back to life. Not while managing four kids doing school from home. Not while trying to stay sober. Something had to give.

So, I walked away.

Not because I stopped caring – but because I finally realized I had to start caring for myself. My focus narrowed to two things: holding my family together, and learning how to live without alcohol.

But sobriety doesn't come without substitutes.

I started replacing rituals that once defined my evenings. The wine glass that was like a fixture in my hand was suddenly gone. But the muscle memory remained. My hands ached for something to hold. So I began drinking tea. So much tea. Herbal, decaf, fruity, spiced. It didn't matter what kind – only that it was warm, grounding, and something I could wrap my fingers around. I was drinking more tea than I ever thought possible. The glass of wine I used to refill without thinking was now a mug of chamomile. The numbing was gone, but something softer took its place.

Evenings were the hardest. The witching hour. That familiar pull toward the couch next to my husband – the same spot I had spent countless nights draining glass after glass of wine under the soft glow of the TV. I couldn't sit there anymore. Not in those early days. Not without the unbearable tug of old habits. So I started retreating upstairs early. Long before the rest of the house wound down. I'd curl into bed with my tea and a book in my hands with the hope that maybe, just maybe, I'd be able to shut my mind off a little sooner that night. This new rhythm felt foreign at first – quiet, lonely, like I was ghosting my own life. But slowly, I realized I wasn't leaving – I was returning. To myself.

Still, even in that quiet retreat, I needed to know I wasn't the only one. I longed for connection – for proof that someone, somewhere, understood.

The unexpected gift of social media was that, in all the noise, there were corners of the internet filled with people like me. Support groups. Sober pages. Strangers sharing their truth. I started reading their posts. Their words. Their stories.

That's when I came across a suggested sobriety app I could download on my phone – one that allowed me to track my progress, day by day. I checked in each morning, recommitting to staying sober and logging each night I hadn't had a drink. It held me accountable. It gave me something to build on. A growing count of days – a quiet, steady reminder that I was doing it. That I was choosing this path, one day at a time.

Soon after, I read a post from someone suggesting the book *This Naked Mind* by Annie Grace – a science-backed, insightful exploration of how alcohol affects the brain and why so many of us become hooked without realizing it. I ordered it and had it in my hands the next day. I devoured it in a single night – desperate to understand why giving up alcohol felt like losing a part of myself and saving myself at the same time. And that's when everything came into sharper focus. I didn't just feel understood – I felt informed.

For the first time, I began to learn what alcohol actually *does* to the brain. How it gives a quick hit of feel-good chemicals – like dopamine – and then just as quickly takes them away. How that sudden rush confuses the brain into thinking it doesn't need to make as much on its own. And how the craving that follows isn't about weak willpower – it's your brain trying to find its balance again.

That truth hit hard. I had already been living with anxiety, so my emotional balance was already shaky. That glass of wine I used to "take the edge off" didn't lift me higher – it just brought me to baseline. And when it wore off, I dropped below that line again. No wonder I craved more. For the first time, I understood why drinking had made me feel *normal* – because it temporarily balanced what already felt out of sync. It wasn't because I was broken. It was because my brain was trying to recalibrate.

Drinking for me wasn't just a habit – it was a trap. A cycle I was biologically primed to repeat. And once I understood that science, I could finally stop seeing myself as someone who simply made bad choices. I wasn't just reckless. I wasn't a mess. I was a human being with a vulnerable nervous system, responding to a substance designed to hijack it.

Learning that truth didn't erase the pain, but it gave me language. It gave me power. And it gave me permission to stop blaming myself.

After that, I began tearing through every book I could find – stories of addiction, recovery, anxiety, healing, faith. I needed voices that echoed the noise in my own head so I wouldn't feel so alone in it. I had never listened to audiobooks before, but I downloaded a few on a whim – and instantly, I was hooked. I started walking every day – miles at a time – earbuds in, heart pounding, fresh air in my lungs, and a spark lit inside me. The rhythm of my feet on the pavement, paired with the steady stream of stories, sent feel-good chemicals rushing through my brain. I was moving. Breathing. Listening. Healing. These books carried me when I couldn't carry myself.

Some pointed me toward the truth – *We Are the Luckiest* and *Quit Like a Woman* cracked me open and helped me name what I hadn't been able to admit. Others – like *Blackout*, *The Sober Diaries*, *Between Breaths*, and *The Highlight Real* – reminded me that I wasn't the only one who had quietly fallen apart under the pressure to look "fine." I underlined pages in *Rewired* and *Rewire Your Anxious Brain* like they were maps – clues to how my mind had been wired for survival, and how it might be wired again for peace. *The Easy Way to Stop Drinking*, *Recovery 2.0*, and *The Sober Survival Guide* gave me tools I didn't even know I needed. And *Untamed* – well, that one gave me permission to want more.

Not long after that, I connected with an acquaintance online named Jen. I don't even remember exactly how we found each other – maybe one of the support pages I had quietly joined. But something clicked. We had both walked hard roads – battles with control, numbing, and patterns that once kept us surviving but not truly living. And through it all, we each leaned on a deep faith that carried us through the darkest places. Jen's faith, especially, was unwavering – strong, rooted, and alive in a way that inspired me deeply. She recommended a spiritual book rooted in Christian teachings, and we made a plan – one chapter a week, taking notes, texting each other our reflections and prayers. It became a kind of sacred rhythm, a thread of hope woven between two people who had never met in person but somehow understood each other deeply.

Jen was a mentor, a guide, a steady voice when I needed it most. I'm not sure she ever fully knew how much those quiet exchanges meant to me – how deeply seen and supported I felt during that fragile season. Her presence echoed what the books had begun to reveal as well – that I wasn't alone in this. That healing wasn't linear, and I didn't have to figure it all out on my own.

The books were anchors in my early sobriety. Page after page, step after step, they steadied me when everything else felt unsteady. They whispered truths I needed to hear: *You're not broken. You're becoming. You're not alone.* Each one felt like a mirror held gently to my face – not to judge, but to remind me of who I still was beneath the unraveling. They weren't just stories – they were confessions, lessons, lifelines. They gave me language for my pain, courage for my healing, and hope that change was possible.

But healing is rarely tidy. As I began to loosen my grip on alcohol, other things rose to the surface. My body, long used to chasing quick comfort, started reaching in new directions. The sugar cravings hit fast and fierce. At first, I laughed them off – ice cream became my nightly ritual, whole pints at a time, the cold sweetness quieting the edge of the day. It felt innocent. Even deserved.

But beneath that ritual, something old and painful stirred. Alongside the comfort came familiar urges I thought I had outgrown. Old thoughts I hadn't heard in years. The seductive voice of bulimia, whispering its rehearsed lies. Promising control. Promising relief.

And I was horrified. I was an adult. A mother of four. I had built a full life. I had moved on. Hadn't I?

I felt so ashamed, gripped by a fear I thought I'd outgrown. How could I still want that escape? I needed to talk to someone – to say it out loud – but the thought of telling a friend, or even my sister, made me shrink. I kept it buried, hoping it would quiet down on its own.

But it didn't. The craving, the ache, the fear – it all kept building. Until finally, the weight of it became too much to carry in silence. I picked up my phone. Just holding it felt like a betrayal of the secrecy I'd clung to. My thumb hovered over the screen. I stared at the number for what felt like hours. Because making that call meant crossing a line I couldn't uncross. It meant asking for help. Admitting I wasn't okay.

But I did. I called Teresa – a doula I had worked with during pregnancy. From the very beginning, Teresa had struck me as one of those rare people who exude calm, kindness, and quiet strength. I had trusted her immediately. She had already seen me in some of the most vulnerable moments of my life – when our baby Cam was breech in my belly and she came to the house, gently guiding me into positions to help him turn naturally. Or the time I was struggling with breastfeeding and she came over without hesitation, using her hands to help relieve the issue, her touch clinical but deeply compassionate. Raw moments. Intimate ones. And she had held them with care. Even though we didn't stay in regular contact, I knew she was someone I could call. Someone far enough removed, yet safe enough to tell the truth.

When I got her on the phone, I told her everything. The drinking. The quitting. The ice cream. The shame. The anxiety. The haunting temptation to return to the disorder I thought I had buried decades ago. I trembled and I cried on that call. These were things I hadn't told anyone before, ever. At the same time that it was nauseating to open up about these secrets, it also was a huge relief.

When I finally found the courage to speak the words aloud – to admit that the old urges had returned, that the pull to binge and purge was creeping back in, subtle but persistent – Teresa didn't flinch. She didn't rush to reassure me or try to fix it. She just listened. Her voice was calm and unwavering, like a lighthouse in a storm. I told her how confusing it felt – how something I thought I had buried long ago was suddenly resurfacing, uninvited. It caught me off guard, like hearing a song I hadn't played in years, and still remembering every word.

And then she said something that settled deep into my bones and never left.

"Picture a mountain," she began, her voice soft and grounded. "One you've climbed over and over again throughout your life. Each time you made that climb, you followed a path – this path represents a coping mechanism that helped you survive. The first path you ever found was bulimia. It was steep, painful, and isolating, but it was yours. You walked it so many times, it wore into the earth like a scar. You knew every rock, every sharp turn. It became instinct – a reflex. A way to disappear when life felt too sharp, too loud, too much. And for a while, that path worked – not because it healed you, but because it numbed you just enough to keep going."

She paused, her words hanging gently in the space between us.

"Later, you discovered another path – alcohol. It was a different trail, but it led to the same place: numbness, relief, a way out of the noise. And eventually, that path became just as familiar."

Her voice stayed soft but certain.

"But now, you've made the choice to stop walking that alcohol path. That's brave. That's massive. But your brain, clever and wired for survival, gets nervous without a clear trail to follow. So it scans the ground – and it spots the old bulimia path, the one that was first etched into your nervous system. It's overgrown now, faded from years of not being used - but it's still there. And your brain, in a voice that almost sounds helpful, says: *'Hey... I know this way. Want to try it again?'*"

"But here's the thing," she said gently. "You don't have to say yes. You can create a new path – one that's unfamiliar now but will grow clearer with every step. And, Vanessa, this phone call to me – this opening up – this is a *huge* first step up a new path. One built on truth. On health. On connection. Keep walking *that* path. Eventually, it becomes the one you trust."

She wasn't judging me. She was naming something true. That when you're in pain, your mind will reach for what it knows – even if what it knows hurts you. Especially if it once helped you survive.

In that moment, I didn't feel shame.

I felt seen.

And that was the beginning of my healing.

Chapter Twelve

Feeling It All

Sobriety cleared the fog. But it didn't bring peace – not right away. Because with the numbing haze of alcohol gone, something else emerged: pain. Sharp. Unrelenting. And unsettlingly familiar – like a shadow I thought I'd outrun. For the first time in years, I was fully inside my body – and it was screaming. Not metaphorically. Literally.

For most of my life, I thought my body was just... strange. Unreliable in ways no one could quite explain. Aches, pains, joints that slipped or strained too easily. Fingers that turned white and numb at the slightest breeze. Knees that throbbed. Hips that felt off. A belly that constantly ached. A heart that fluttered too fast. And as I got older, my legs – always heavy, always aching. Veins that bulged and throbbed, pulsing with discomfort I had learned to normalize.

As a child, my mom had taken me from doctor to doctor, hoping someone could connect the dots. But the answers were always vague, almost dismissive: probably nothing serious. Try this. Try that. Learn to live with it. So I did. I learned to smile through the discomfort, to try every new supplement or stretch or brace, to schedule another massage, another adjustment. I carried the quiet belief that maybe I was just dramatic. Maybe I was imagining it.

But when I got sober, everything changed. Without the haze of alcohol numbing my nervous system, without the nightly ritual of pouring glass after glass of wine to smooth out the edges, I began to feel everything more clearly. The pain, the stiffness, the dull ache I used to drown out at the end of the day? It was no longer muted. It roared. The joint pain, once background noise, suddenly screamed its presence. It woke me in the middle of the night. It flared up after the smallest tasks. It was like my body had been whispering to me for years – and now, without alcohol turning down the volume, I finally heard it. And it was unbearable.

I started seeking relief, but in a healthier way. A different path up that mountain. This wasn't about managing pain so I could function – it was about surviving each day without feeling like I was being swallowed by it. I tried everything: massage, supplements, bodywork, adjustments. And through it all, I'm pretty sure my sister – the ever-patient RN – was ready to block my number, fielding my near-daily texts and calls asking her to help me decode every strange twinge, sharp pain, or flare-up.

In the pursuit of relief, I booked an appointment with a new chiropractor – hoping for something, anything, to ease the ache. Midway through the session, he paused. He looked at me – really looked at me – and gently asked, "Has anyone ever mentioned the possibility of a connective tissue disorder?" I blinked, confused. "No," I said. "Why?" He explained. Slowly. Kindly. "They're rare, and not always well understood," he said. "But I've worked with patients who have something called Ehlers-Danlos Syndrome – specifically the hypermobile type. And... well, you present with a lot of similar symptoms."

My ears perked up, but my mind brushed it off. Another condition to add to my long list. Another label I probably didn't need to go Googling. I filed it away and left, not thinking much more of it.

Then, a few weeks later, I saw a friend's post. She was sharing her story – her health, her struggles, her body that never quite behaved. I couldn't believe the similarities. Symptom after symptom mirrored my own. And then there it was again: *Ehlers-Danlos*. I froze. I read the post again, slower this time, letting each word sink in like puzzle pieces finally falling into place.

Her story sounded so much like mine. The odd symptoms. The random, scattered diagnoses. The constant feeling that something was wrong – but never having the language to explain it. I reached out to her, and we ended up talking in detail. She told me how long it took to get answers. How validating it was to finally hear she wasn't imagining it. That she wasn't crazy. That there was a reason.

And after sharing our similar experiences, she said, "You should see a geneticist." It felt like a breadcrumb trail I hadn't even realized I was following – suddenly lit up, pointing me forward. So I did. I made the appointments. I sat through the evaluations. I answered questions I didn't even know mattered – about flexibility, chronic pain, fatigue, dizziness, old injuries, dental issues, and more. It was like someone was finally making sense of my entire medical history.

And then, finally, came the diagnosis: Hypermobile Ehlers-Danlos Syndrome. The geneticist explained it gently but clearly. Ehlers-Danlos is a group of connective tissue disorders – and connective tissue is everywhere in the body - it holds it all together: skin, joints, blood vessels, even internal organs. When that tissue is too loose or fragile, like in the hypermobile type, it can cause a wide range of symptoms that seem unrelated but all trace back to the same source. And suddenly, my lifetime of scattered symptoms made sense.

The joint pain. The hip brace. The racing heart. The surgeries. The Raynaud's. The veins. The stomach issues. All of it – connected.

It wasn't random. It wasn't imagined. And even though there's no cure, no one-size-fits-all treatment, the diagnosis gave me something I hadn't had before: validation. Permission to stop apologizing for what my body had always known. Permission to stop feeling like a burden.

I wasn't lazy or fragile or difficult. I was living with a real condition – one that had quietly shaped so much of my life. One I had unknowingly tried to manage with alcohol – to numb the anxiety, to dull the pain, to make everything feel just a little more bearable. The diagnosis didn't erase the pain, but it gave it meaning. It offered grace. For the first time, I could say: This isn't my fault. I'm not broken. And I'm not alone.

The clarity was validating – but it didn't bring instant relief. Yes, I finally had a name for why my body felt like it was always working against me. But the emotional weight – all those years of pushing through, of blaming myself, of numbing instead of listening – didn't just disappear.

For so long, I believed if just one thing changed – the right diagnosis, the right job, the right solution – maybe I'd finally feel okay. But healing doesn't come from fixing or finding. It comes from surrender. From slowing down. From finally turning toward the pain instead of away from it.

And that's where the next chapter of my journey began – with another small, steady step upward on a path I was still learning to trust.

Chapter Thirteen

Beginning Again

Once I had a name for what was happening in my body, I thought I'd feel better. Lighter, maybe. Freed by the truth. And in some ways, I did. But clarity isn't the same as comfort.

The diagnosis explained the pain – but it didn't quiet the noise. It didn't soothe the anxiety still pulsing under my skin. It didn't change the fact that I was now standing fully sober, emotionally exposed, with nothing left to numb me. And by then, the anxiety was deafening. The racing thoughts. The restlessness. That constant sense of dread, like something terrible was just around the corner – even when everything on the outside looked fine. I was exhausted from trying to hold it all together on my own.

That's when I thought back to the call with the doula – the one that shifted something deep inside me. The one where I finally said the hard thing out loud: *I'm not okay*. There was no collapse, no dramatic breakdown. Just a quiet moment of truth with someone who didn't try to fix me. She simply listened. And reminded me: healing begins when we stop hiding.

That was it. The beginning. A small, unsteady step toward something new. Not a grand plan – just the next right thing. From there, I made two appointments: one with my primary care, and one with a therapist. I didn't even know what I would say – only that I needed to say something. I couldn't keep carrying the fear, the shame, the exhaustion alone anymore. It was time to stop pretending I was fine.

At those first appointments, I made myself a promise: *no more hiding*. I told my doctor everything – how it felt like I was always on edge, always spiraling, how even the smallest things left me overwhelmed. We went over my full medical history, and I finally spoke out loud the things I had only ever whispered to myself: the restlessness, the racing thoughts, the tightness in my chest that never seemed to leave. I explained how groups unnerved me – how being in a room where attention might turn toward me, even momentarily, could send my nervous system into overdrive. My heart would race, my breath would catch, my palms would sweat, my thoughts would tangle. On the outside, I looked composed. But inside, it felt like an alarm I couldn't turn off.

I told her something else I had never said out loud before – that whether I was doing something simple, like parking my car, or something more complex, like navigating a situation with the kids, my mind would run through every possible worst-case scenario. It was automatic. Constant. A background hum of dread that I had learned to live with. I thought everyone's mind worked that way – always scanning, always bracing, always preparing to manage the worst. I didn't realize it was anxiety. I thought it was just being responsible.

She listened closely, then said gently, "What you're experiencing is a disorder. And what you just described is something called catastrophizing – it's part of that. Your brain is working so hard to protect you, but it's stuck in overdrive. Let's help it find balance again."

And just like that, it finally had a name – or two, actually: Generalized Anxiety Disorder and Social Anxiety Disorder. They weren't new. I had been carrying them for years, silently and unknowingly, without the language to name them or the support to treat them. I had learned to manage in the only ways I knew how – ways that dulled the edges just enough to function. But those ways came at a cost. And now, without numbing, I was left to face what had always been there. Not as a personal failing, but as a call for care – one I had spent years trying to silence.

So we began. Anxiety medication wasn't instant. It wasn't magic. It was slow, frustrating, and messy. There were so many options. Different types. Different doses. Each new prescription carried the hope that maybe this one would help. But every trial required weeks – sometimes months – to adjust, to monitor side effects, to see if anything was actually shifting. I tried one. Then another. Then combinations. I was exhausted from hoping. From waiting. From wondering if it would ever get easier.

But I kept going.

Because alongside the medication, there was therapy. And therapy – while not easy – was the steady hand I didn't know I'd been reaching for. I had been on a waitlist for a long time – like so many others during the pandemic – all of us trying to hold it together while quietly falling apart. But when I finally got in, I was matched with Queen – and she truly lived up to her name. With a presence that felt both grounded and sacred, she held space for me in a way no one else ever had. She was sharp, perceptive, unwavering – like royalty in her wisdom and calm. Queen didn't just listen; she offered real-time coping strategies that worked. Tangible tools. Gentle challenges. Reframes that shifted everything. I can't say enough about her. I still refer everyone I know to her – anyone who's struggling, anyone who needs someone steady and true.

The work we did together was amazing... and brutal. I opened up about things I hadn't said out loud in years – and some I had never said at all. Childhood fears. Anxiety. Teenage heartbreak. Bulimia. Alcohol. Loneliness. Trauma.

Some sessions left me shaky for hours. Others had to end early because I couldn't get through the tears. There were days I walked out feeling lighter, more understood. And there were days I left feeling like I had been turned inside out. But I kept showing up. Finally. Slowly. For real.

And somewhere in the middle of all that rawness, I realized something: talk therapy and medication weren't enough on their own. I needed something to hold me in the in-between moments – the space between appointments, between meds kicking in, between the pain and the healing.

That's when yoga re-entered my life. The idea returned like a whisper – a quiet invitation. I had practiced it on and off for many years – but always as exercise. A way to sweat, to tone, to try to control my body. This time, it was going to mean something different. I didn't know exactly what it was going to offer me – only that I needed it. Something in me was ready to try again.

I started at home – just me and a screen, squeezing in short flows while the kids were logged in to virtual school, rolling out my mat in the living room while our Golden, Gracie, treated it like a game. She'd jump up on me during standing warrior poses, crawl underneath me and slobber my face in downward dog – like yoga was our shared playtime, not my moment of peace. But her joy, her steadiness, her constant affection were healing in their own right. Gracie reminded me, in ways words never could, what unconditional love feels like – softening the edges of even my hardest days. It wasn't the peaceful practice I imagined, but it gave me something real. For those brief moments, I remembered how it felt to be in my body. Not trying to change it. Just trying to be in it.

Still, it didn't take long to realize I needed more. I needed space – physical and emotional – away from the house, away from the noise. A place where Gracie wasn't pouncing on me mid-pose or trying to lick my face every time I hit the floor, where laundry didn't stare at me from the corner, and no one needed snacks or help with homework. I needed a room that wasn't mine. A place where I wasn't mom or wife. Just a woman trying to breathe.

That's when I found a small studio within walking distance from my house. It felt like a blessing. They had just reopened with stickers on the floor to keep us six feet apart and masks on our faces – but I didn't care. I would have practiced in a hazmat suit if it meant I could feel what I felt in that room. For the first time in a long time, I found relief. Something real. Something steady.

Yoga gave me access to something I hadn't known how to find on my own: peace. Not the kind you earn by being good or getting everything right – but the kind that lives quietly inside you when you finally stop running.

When I had practiced yoga before, I didn't understand that it had so much more to offer than just a stronger core or better posture. But now, in this season of rawness and rebuilding, I returned not for my body, but for my soul. This time, it was about breathing through discomfort instead of numbing it. About grounding myself when anxiety tried to pull me under. About learning to be still, to be present, to feel everything – and still be safe. Yoga became the quiet space where I could cry without explanation, shake without shame, and begin to trust my body again – not as something to control or punish, but as something worthy of compassion.

I didn't know it then, but this wasn't just about healing – it was about transformation. A new path. A soulful one. One that didn't lead away from myself, but back home. I was learning new ways to cope. Healthier ways. Slower ways.

VANESSA FRANCE

Ways that didn't require punishing or disappearing. I wasn't just trying to survive anymore – I was truly starting to heal.

And healing, I've learned, isn't linear. It's full of setbacks, second-guessing, and starting over. It's a thousand small choices to keep going, even when it feels impossible. But it always begins the same way: with one moment of truth. One conversation. One whispered *I need help*. That's what I had finally given myself.

The terrain was still steep. But I was learning a new way forward – slower, steadier, more honest. With each breath, each uncurled fist, each quiet return to the mat, I wasn't just building a practice. I was learning how to stay.

Chapter Fourteen

Learning to Stay

Getting sober changed everything. Not just for me – but for *us*.

For years, alcohol had been my off switch – my escape hatch when things got tense, when arguments flared, when I felt too much. I thought if I removed the wine, the fog would clear and everything else would fall into place. But real sobriety? It meant facing the feelings I'd spent so long avoiding. It meant staying.

And for the first time in our marriage, I had to actually feel things. I had to remain in the heat of the moment without retreating into a buzz. I had to sit through discomfort instead of numbing it.

It was foreign. And it was hard.

Matt had married one version of me – the woman who held her own at parties, poured the wine, kept everything moving. And yes, he saw the drinking. He saw the cracks beginning to show. But did he really know how deep it ran? Not really. No one did. Not even him.

He knew I'd pour a drink before we went out – just to calm my nerves. That part wasn't hidden. But he didn't notice how often I refilled it. How the glass never really emptied. He didn't see the bargaining that played out in my mind each night – the quiet countdown to bedtime so I could pour another, the silent negotiations about how much was "too much," the way I'd sneak one last shot from his bottle after he'd gone upstairs. So when I started telling people I was sober, I watched the disbelief ripple across their faces. *You?* or *I didn't realize it was that bad.* They meant it. And I believed them.

Because I'd become so good at pretending everything was fine. But my husband had seen more than most. He had lived with the tension. The excuses. The empty conversations where everything important went unsaid. And now the numbing was gone. There we were – just us. Two people who had built a life together, who were raising four children, who had weathered joys and storms side by side – suddenly faced with learning each other all over again. Because I had been checking out for years. Now I was trying to learn how to stay. To feel. To process. To talk. And God, was that messy…

I didn't know how to have hard conversations without going cold or getting defensive. I didn't know how to cry without apologizing. I didn't know how to let myself be seen – not without the numbing haze I'd relied on for so long. And he – he did his best. He was patient. Kind. Confused. Frustrated. Supportive. Worn out. He didn't sign up for this version of me. He fell into it.

Still, under all that effort – his and mine – lived a quieter fear: if I kept choosing sobriety while he was still drinking, would our lives still move in the same direction? There were nights I couldn't even sit in the same spot on the couch where we used to drink together – not when he still could, and I no longer did. I didn't want to change him. I just didn't know how to hold the difference without losing us.

And there were moments – so many moments – when I wondered if it was still fair. If he'd still choose me now that I wasn't the *fun one*, the laid-back one, the woman who could shrug things off with a laugh and a glass in her hand. That version of me had been easier to be around. Easier to love, maybe. She didn't rock the boat. She didn't cry at the kitchen sink or need space to regulate her nervous system.

But I wasn't her anymore. And the truth was, I didn't know who I was yet. That was the scariest part. Sobriety stripped everything down to the bone. It didn't just ask me to stop drinking – it demanded I look at everything I had avoided while using it. It forced me to rebuild from the inside out, and not just myself, but the way I showed up in our marriage, in motherhood, in every relationship I had ever molded myself to fit into.

And the truth is, I'm still learning. There are still days I want to bolt – to disappear into distraction, to chase the numbness that used to keep the pain quiet. But now, I stay. I don't leave the room – not physically, not emotionally. I don't reach for something to take the edge off. I let myself feel the sting. I sit in the discomfort. I speak – imperfectly, awkwardly, sometimes tearfully – but I speak. And every time I do, I build something real. Not perfect. Not polished. But something true.

I used to think love meant smoothing over the hard parts, swallowing the words, pretending everything was fine. Now I know that real love is forged in the fire – in the misunderstandings, the vulnerability, the willingness to stay in the difficult moments when it would be easier to walk away. Real love is showing up anyway. Eyes open. Hand outstretched, ready to catch the other if they slip. A quiet promise: *wait for me, and I'll wait for you.*

When I look back, I don't just see the version of me who numbed her way through the discomfort – who kept everything light and easy so she wouldn't have to feel the weight. I see the woman who finally stopped running. Who stayed. Who learned to tell the truth. First to herself. Then to the people she loved.

And maybe, most importantly, I see the man who stayed with her while she learned how.

Chapter Fifteen

The Mat That Carried Me Home

S taying was one thing. Learning how to stay was another entirely.

Sobriety stripped away the distractions and left me face-to-face with everything I used to outrun – the tension, the discomfort, the aching vulnerability of being fully present. I was learning how to show up in my relationships, how to tell the truth, how to feel without numbing. But even as I stayed – in the room, in the conversation, in my body – I often didn't know what to do with all I was feeling.

There, yoga found me.

Not in some grand epiphany, but in the quiet, almost accidental rhythm of unrolling my mat. Again and again, day after day. At first, a lot was focused on the movement – a way to stretch, to exhale, to settle my frayed nerves. Over time, though, it became something deeper – a rhythm, a refuge, a way to hold steady when everything in me still wanted to run.

Yoga became more than movement – it became my sanctuary. The one place where I didn't have to perform or explain. Where I could be fully present, fully real, and maybe for the first time, fully held. Not by another person – but by myself. By the breath. By the healing rhythm of the practice. By the space I created each time I whispered *yes* to healing, even when it hurt. There was something ancient in it. Something remembering. Each time I pressed my palms together at my heart or folded forward in surrender, it felt less like exercise and more like returning – not to who I had been, but to who I was becoming.

There was one instructor in particular, Emily, who unlocked something sacred in me. She likely had no idea how deeply I cherished her classes, how desperately I clung to those quiet hours as if they were oxygen. The way she guided us through each pose wasn't just physical – it was emotional, even spiritual. She invited me to listen – not just to my body, but to the buried corners of my being, where pain and grief still lived. Where fear still hid.

Every savasana ended with a soft reading – always gentle, always poetic, always somehow exactly what I needed. And almost every time, I cried. Not from sadness. But from release. Tears slid down silently, without drama or apology – as if my body finally had permission to feel everything I had buried for so long.

One evening, as we lay still in the quiet glow of closing practice, Emily read a passage from Mark Nepo's *The Book of Awakening*, called "The Courage of the Seed." A few lines echoed in my chest long after class ended:

"All the buried seeds crack open in the dark the instant they surrender to a process they can't see."

I remember lying there, heart thudding, overcome with a feeling I couldn't name – and something in *me* cracked open too. That image stayed with me. It didn't feel like a metaphor – it felt like recognition. Like the truth I'd been circling but couldn't quite touch.

Maybe I wasn't falling apart. Maybe I was *beginning*.

That reading planted something deep in me – a quiet knowing that healing doesn't come from holding it all together, but from surrendering. From cracking open to the light. From trusting the process, even when you can't see the outcome. That was the moment I began to understand: sharing my story wasn't just brave – it was necessary.

In the beginning, I had marked my sobriety milestones in silence – one week, one month, three months. I kept them tucked close to my chest, too ashamed to let the world in on how bad it had been. But something shifted; that seed of knowing took root. As I moved deeper into recovery, each milestone felt less like a secret and more like a quiet miracle.

Eventually, I began to say it aloud. First to a few trusted people. Then, more publicly. Each time I said the words – *I'm sober* – it felt like taking my power back, like stepping out from behind the curtain of shame.

At 100 days, the milestone felt monumental – exhilarating and a little daunting. Around that same time, I saw a post from an old friend – a talented photographer – sharing some of her recent work. Something in me lit up. I hadn't had portraits taken since school, and the idea of marking this season in that way felt both terrifying and thrilling. So I booked a session with her.

I wanted her to capture what I could feel radiating from my sober body – a quiet glow, steady and unforced. And she did. But it wasn't just the photos. It was the way she saw me – how her lens reflected back the strength and softness I was only beginning to recognize in myself. When the images came back, I was so proud to share them – and to share my sobriety with the world.

And I kept sharing – other days, other markers, the quiet wins that stitched themselves into a life. I wrote about it, posted reflections, let the truth breathe outside of me. With each telling, something lifted. It was freeing. Empowering. A beginning, again and again.

What happened next stunned me. People reached out – old classmates, former coworkers, even distant acquaintances. They thanked me. They admitted they were struggling too. They said my story made them feel less alone, that it gave them hope.

That's when I realized something deeply beautiful: telling the truth doesn't just set you free – it opens a door for others, too. With each passing day, the fog lifted a little more. In that light, I could see my actual life more clearly – maybe for the first time – and it was beautiful.

Messy, yes. Imperfect, always. But real.

As I kept returning to the mat, I realized something else: yoga wasn't just holding me together anymore – it was calling me forward.

I started to pay closer attention to the instructors guiding those classes – especially Emily. There was something in the way she held space, in the way her words landed at just the right time, like she was speaking directly to the parts of me I was just beginning to uncover. And I began to wonder: *what if I could offer that presence too? What if I could help someone feel seen in the way I had?*

Quietly, I began looking into yoga teacher training. I wasn't ready to tell anyone yet – it felt too tender, too new. I searched online late at night, reading about different programs and what they required. Anatomy, philosophy, practicum hours... it felt both intimidating and electrifying. And as if the universe – or more likely the algorithm – had caught wind of my secret longing, teacher training ads started showing up on my social media feeds. Over and over again. Little nudges I couldn't ignore.

So I enrolled – not because I had everything figured out, but because something in me knew: this was the next right step. Another foothold on that new path up the mountain.

***

It was the height of COVID, so everything was virtual – an unexpected blessing, since my days were already a delicate dance of remote-schooling four kids, juggling masked-up half-days and Zoom school from the kitchen table. Still, I dove in. I ordered every book, downloaded every manual, and studied late into the night. I was ravenous for it – soaking up every word, every lesson, every ancient thread of wisdom.

That hunger for understanding found direction when I opened the Yoga Sutras for the first time. It felt like the pages had been written just for me – a roadmap back to myself. When I reached the yamas and niyamas, I paused. These weren't just rules to follow – they were invitations. Invitations to live with more honesty, more compassion, more steadiness. They spoke directly to the parts of me shaped by fear – the parts that hustled for worth, that molded themselves to fit in, that were terrified of rejection.

A few stood out right away. *Ahimsa* – non-harming – asked me to soften the way I spoke to myself, to stop punishing my body and mind for struggling. *Satya* – truthfulness – nudged me to stop hiding, to tell the truth even when it trembled out of me. And *tapas* – the discipline of inner fire – reminded me that healing isn't always gentle. Sometimes it requires grit. Commitment. The willingness to stay, even when it's hard.

Integrating them wasn't instant. It was clumsy and humbling – the slow unlearning of habits that had once protected me but were now keeping me stuck.

Saying no without apology. Resting without guilt. Holding space for discomfort without rushing to numb it. But over time, they became part of me – a new kind of compass. They taught me how to stay with myself – not just on the mat, but in the messy middle of everyday life.

And still, along the way, anxiety crept in – whispering doubts about whether I was actually capable of learning all of this, let alone sharing it with others. My mind would loop through worst-case scenarios: *What if I forgot something important? What if I taught it wrong? What if I didn't know enough?* That pressure grew loudest when it came to things like learning the Sanskrit names for every pose – at first, I believed I had to get it all perfect before I could even consider teaching. The weight of that expectation was overwhelming.

But little by little, I began to realize something deeper: yoga is a practice. Not a performance. Not a test. It is a lifelong return to center – imperfect, evolving, and deeply human. I didn't need to know it all. I just needed to begin. My life would be the evidence of that practice – always learning, always returning.

As I dove deeper into the other limbs of yoga, everything inside me settled. It was like finding a language for what I had already begun to live. These weren't just teachings; they were a framework for wholeness – for living awake, connected, and anchored in something deeper than the chaos of circumstance. It was no longer just about what happened on the mat – it was about how I moved through the world. How I listened. How I responded. How I returned to center when life pulled me off course.

The more I studied, the more I knew: this wasn't just something I practiced. This was the path I was meant to walk. To live. To share.

That quiet knowing began to take shape in new ways. I found myself drawn not only to the wisdom of yoga, but to its healing potential – especially for those silently carrying anxiety and overwhelm, as I had for so long. So I also enrolled in a specialized certification in Yoga Therapy for Anxiety, eager to understand how movement, breath, and mindfulness could help regulate the nervous system and bring people back to themselves, one steady exhale at a time.

The more I learned, the more it became clear: this wasn't just about me anymore. Healing had opened a door I hadn't even known was closed – and on the other side were others traveling their own winding paths. I didn't know it then, but I wouldn't step through alone.

Chapter Sixteen

Answering The Call

Yoga had become my anchor – a lifeline woven from breath, presence, and quiet resilience during a season marked by uncertainty. But what surprised me most was not the strength I found in my body, but the depth of connection it quietly opened in my life.

Two women, in particular, would go on to change everything.

There was something about practicing beside Rebekah that grounded me – a steady calm in her presence that made the space feel safe. Her energy had always felt familiar, like a kindred spirit. I had admired her from afar for a while, drawn to her quiet confidence, her grace, and the way she carried herself with strength that didn't need to be loud to be felt. She was a fellow mom of four, which only deepened the sense of connection – an unspoken understanding of the beautiful chaos we both navigated daily.

One evening after class, we struck up a conversation as we rolled up our mats, still wrapped in the glow of savasana. Between laughter and shared stories, we discovered we were both enrolled in teacher training. Neither of us had known.

We laughed in that serendipitous way that makes you believe the universe had been nudging you together all along.

Around that same time, I often found myself lingering after class to chat with one of our most beloved instructors – Timea. A local realtor with a big heart and a glow of grounded joy. I looked up to her more than she probably knew. There was something about the way she led – full of passion, grit, and positivity – that made me believe in what was possible. On many of those nights, I would open up about my sobriety, unsure if I was oversharing. But she always met me with warmth and honesty. She would share pieces of her own wellness journey, and somehow, our conversations felt like light in a dark room. She believed in me. And at a time when I was still learning to believe in myself, that meant everything.

It was during this season of quiet connection and personal growth that something unexpected happened. The studio's owner shared, almost in passing, that she was planning to retire and sell the business. With four young kids, the idea of taking it on felt wild. Unrealistic. But a question stirred in me – *what if I didn't have to do it alone?*

By then, I'd begun forming meaningful connections with those two incredible women – Rebekah and Timea. We shared more than a love for yoga; we shared a love for movement, nature, and healing. We started meeting at the lake in town to paddleboard, where our time on the water naturally gave way to deeper conversations and an unexpected but steadily growing friendship.

The idea of taking on the studio had been circling for a while – but it was out there on the water, during those quiet afternoons, that it began to take real shape. On our own, it might have felt overwhelming. But the three of us, together? Suddenly, it felt possible.

One afternoon, we found ourselves out on the lake, our boards gliding effortlessly across the glassy water. The sun wrapped us in warmth, and the world around us felt suspended in stillness. As we moved together through that tender space, something inside each of us softened. Words came – honest, unfiltered – and we began to share things we hadn't spoken aloud before. Pieces of our stories, our fears, our hopes. And slowly, that shared vision began to crystallize – not just a dream, but a direction. What once felt uncertain started to feel like alignment – like the beginning of something real.

The lake held it all. The rhythm of the water beneath us, the openness of the sky above, and the safe circle between us created something we couldn't name – only feel. A kind of magic. A remembering. A knowing.

By the time we paused, boards side by side in the middle of the lake, we didn't need to say much more. We looked at each other and just knew: we were meant to build something beautiful together. Something rooted in healing, honesty, and heart. Something sacred. That moment on the water solidified the quiet *yes* already forming in each of us. Three women, each on her own path of becoming. Three lives shaped by pain, softened by grace, and stirred by purpose. This wasn't just an idea – it was a calling.

And somehow, everything aligned. We were all in. All dreaming of something more. What followed were countless conversations, late-night texts, soul-searching, and more than a few spreadsheets we combed through together – crunching numbers, imagining possibilities, mapping out what this could become. We listened. We trusted. And we moved forward – not impulsively, but with clarity, commitment, and heart.

We weren't just opening a studio. We were stepping into something bigger than us.

We knew from the start that if we were going to do this, it had to mean something. The name mattered. We didn't want anything flashy or trendy – we wanted something simple, yet powerful. Grounded. Intentional. When we landed on the word *Zen*, it just felt right. By definition, zen speaks to a state of calm attentiveness – rooted in presence, clarity, and a sense of peace and mindfulness. That was exactly what we hoped to offer – not just a place to move, but a place to breathe, to return, to come home to yourself.

We called it *Zen Yoga & Wellness* because we knew it wouldn't be just about the physical practice. It would be more. A space for healing, connection, rest, and renewal. A place where the full spectrum of wellness could live – body, mind, and spirit.

And so, on December 31, 2021, we reopened the doors to our beloved studio – rebranded, reshaped, and infused with our hearts.

I still remember the feeling of unlocking that door for the first time as an owner. My hand on the key. My heart pounding. It was surreal – wild and beautiful and terrifying in the very best way. That door didn't just open to a studio – it opened to a new chapter of my life. One where I wasn't escaping anymore. I was building. Rooting. Growing. It felt, without a doubt, like fate had led me there.

And I wasn't doing it alone. The two women I get to call my business partners have become more like sisters. I love and respect them both deeply – for their strength, their vision, their hearts. Walking this path with them has been one of the greatest gifts of all.

Together, we've poured ourselves into this studio – heart, soul, sweat, and faith. We've expanded to a second location. Launched international wellness retreats. Held space for thousands of students walking through our doors with stories, pain, longing, and hope. We've built something real. Something meaningful.

And we haven't done it alone.

Within our studio walls, we are endlessly blessed with an incredible team of instructors – each one knowledgeable, unique, and deeply committed in their own way. They bring their whole hearts to every class, every student, every moment. They are the light of the studio – illuminating the path with wisdom, warmth, and presence.

At the heart of it all is our community – the people who walk through our doors every day and breathe life into this space. The mothers, the healers, the seekers, the ones in quiet pain, and the ones finding joy again. They show up with courage and vulnerability, with laughter and tears. They are the heartbeat of the studio. Their trust, their energy, their willingness to show up – it all means more than I can say. This community has become a second family.

And like all true families, it began to shape us – stretching our vision, deepening our purpose, calling us to dream even bigger. What began as a shared hope between a few hearts has become something far greater. Zen is no longer just a name – it's a living, breathing reminder of what's possible when people come together to heal.

Out of that foundation, one of the most exciting chapters is unfolding: we're preparing to launch our very own Yoga Teacher Training program at Zen – a dream born from everything this community has become. I feel both proud and deeply humbled to help others step onto this path – to grow as teachers, leaders, and space holders within the same walls that once held so much of my own transformation. In many ways, it feels like the calling that began on the water that day has only grown louder – not just mine to carry, but ours to share.

And just as we've grown deeper roots within our studio walls, we've also stretched our wings outward, beyond them. Our retreats have carried us to the red rocks of Sedona, the turquoise waters of Turks and Caicos – and soon to the lush rainforests of Costa Rica and the sun-drenched coast of Greece. Each one is a deep exhale from the noise. A sacred pause. A remembering. They bring me back to those early sober days – raw and tender. We move. We rest. We nourish our bodies and souls. We laugh. We cry. We let go. And somehow, in that release, we remember who we really are. We come home to ourselves.

Each time I witness someone else come home to themselves, I'm reminded why I kept going. Why I kept choosing this path, even when it was hard. These classes and retreats aren't just moments carved out of busy lives – they're safe harbors. Spaces to set down what we've carried too long, to remember we were never meant to walk alone, and to rise – not just restored, but reshaped. Softer. Stronger. More whole than before.

Perhaps the greatest gift of all is this: that what once felt like the end of me became the beginning of something purposeful.

Yoga didn't just help me recover – it gave me a way to serve. To show up. To hold space for others the way it once held space for me. This journey, this studio, this community – it has become the living, breathing embodiment of letting go and beginning again. And every time I step onto my mat, every time I open the studio doors, I remember: healing doesn't happen in isolation. It happens together, in the spaces where we are seen, supported, and reminded of our worth. That's what Zen has become. And that's the path I'll keep walking – one breath, one step, one genuine offering at a time.

Chapter Seventeen

The Messy, Miraculous Middle

From the outside, it might've looked like everything had come together – a thriving studio, a growing community, a life reshaped with intention and care. But healing doesn't arrive with a tidy bow. It's not a destination – not a finish line you cross and leave behind. It's something I live and breathe now – not just in the studio, but at home with my family. On vacation. In conversation with a friend. I no longer wear different masks to match the moment. I am one person – whole, present, and still becoming.

Even as beautiful things took root around me, the deeper work within me kept unfolding – and still does. What many don't see is the quiet effort that healing still asks of me – in ways both visible and invisible. On and off the mat.

Even now, years into sobriety and recovery, my anxiety lingers. Some days, it hums beneath the surface. Other days, it roars. Before I teach a class, I often need to take medication just to keep panic at bay. For a long time, that felt like failure – like I should've healed past this. I felt that needing help meant I wasn't strong enough, or hadn't worked hard enough. But I see it differently now. It's not weakness – it's wisdom. It's not a step backward – it's a sign that I know what I need to stay calm. That I've learned how to care for the parts of me that still tremble. It's honoring the tools that let me keep showing up with steadiness and care.

That understanding softened something in me. I stopped asking, *What's wrong with me?* and started asking, *What do I need to feel safe?* I no longer saw myself as damaged – I began to see myself as deeply sensitive, and beautifully human. And that shift changed everything: how I speak to my students, how I guide them back to their breath, how I hold space – not with perfection, but with presence and empathy.

Layered into all of it is the reality of living in a body with a connective tissue disorder – a condition that quietly shapes the way I move through the world. Some days, my joints ache without warning. Other days, it's my stomach. Or a strange, shifting pain that defies explanation but feels deeply real. For years, I blamed myself. I thought my body was unreliable – fragile, inconsistent, something to fix. Now, I understand it differently. My body isn't broken – it's just built differently. And it's worthy of support, not shame.

That shift changed the way I show up to teach. Sometimes I'm carrying pain no one can see, or moving carefully to avoid aggravating a joint. I'm not showing up as someone who has it all together – I'm showing up as someone who understands what it means to live in a body that doesn't always cooperate. Who knows how vulnerable it can feel to walk into a yoga class with an injury, a syndrome, a diagnosis. And that's exactly why I'm here. To remind people they don't have to fix or perform or push through. They can meet themselves exactly where they are. Just like I do. Just like I've learned to.

But it's not only my body that holds stories. The deeper layers – the emotional echoes, the old coping patterns – live in me too. No matter how far I've come, there are still tender places – patterns that sometimes try to pull me back in. Sometimes, something small will stir something big – a certain smell, a passing comment, a moment of stillness I didn't ask for – and suddenly, I feel the old ache return. The whisper I thought I'd buried: *just one drink*. It doesn't shout, but it still knows how to find me. I don't follow it anymore. But I don't pretend it isn't there. I acknowledge it. I breathe through it. And I remind myself: it's not about the drink. It's about the ache underneath.

Other times, it's not alcohol that calls to me – it's food. Or rather, the voice that tells me to control it. To shrink. To skip the fat. To "*be good*." That familiar urge to tally, restrict, manage. I've had to learn – and relearn – that food is not the problem, and fat is not the enemy. That I don't need to question the cellulite on my legs or the soft bulge of my belly to determine my worth. When those thoughts creep in now, I pause. I don't ask what I'm craving – I ask what I'm needing. And almost always, it isn't food – it's comfort, grounding, rest, reassurance, permission to feel safe in my own skin.

And that pause matters even more now, because there are little eyes watching. I want my children to know that food is fuel – that their bodies deserve nourishment, joy, and balance, fat and carbs and all of it, in harmony. That worth isn't measured by how small we become, but by how fully we live.

Control had been a theme threaded through so many parts of my story – not just with food, but with how I let myself be seen. Even my once-wild, curly hair became part of the healing. For years I had tamed what was unruly and free, flattening it into something smaller, smoother, quieter – as if I could hide the parts of me I feared were too much. Letting my curls return wasn't just about style. It was about softness. Surrender. It was a quiet act of trust – a daily decision to show up as I am and believe that what's naturally mine is already enough.

That small, outward shift mirrored a much deeper one – the permission to stop fighting myself and start meeting the tender parts of me with compassion. That choice – to stop hiding, to let something naturally expressive remain untamed – began to change how I held space for others. It reminded me that my presence, not my perfection, is what matters most.

I don't show up to teach because I've got it all together – I show up because I don't. Because I still wake up with anxiety. Because old cravings still knock. Because I know what it means to keep coming back to yourself, even when it's hard. I stand at the front of the room not as a polished version of healing, but as someone who still wrestles, still wonders, still returns. And maybe that's the whole point – not to arrive, but to keep coming back.

All of this – the cravings, the control, the pain, the surrender – shapes how I lead. I don't just teach poses. I teach nervous systems how to settle. I teach breath not as performance, but as a way home. I help others embrace who they are – because I've had to learn to do the same. Not because I've mastered peace, but because I know chaos. I've lived it. I've clawed my way back from it. And I still meet it sometimes, even now. And maybe that's the most honest kind of leadership there is.

And yet, even with all that I've learned, the old voice still returns – the one that whispers, *Who do you think you are? Are you really good enough to be leading this?* When it does, I meet it with something new: grace. I don't argue with it. I don't pretend it's not there. I don't push it down. I breathe through it. I return to my mat. And I carry one of the most important mantras I've ever known: *I am enough.*

It's not just for me. I say it in class. I weave it into meditations, into the silence between poses. Because I know I'm not the only one who hears that voice. I know how many others walk through our studio doors carrying that same quiet question in their hearts: *Am I enough?* And I want them to know – I want them to feel the answer not just in words, but in presence – in the safety of the space, in the steadiness of their breath.

Yes, you are.

Even now.

Especially now.

And maybe, just maybe, that's what real healing looks like – not erasing the ache, but learning to stand steady inside it.

Chapter Eighteen

Anchored in Faith

Long before the mat. Before the breathwork. Before the sobriety milestones and the silent savasanas where I cried tears of release – there was one presence that never wavered: my faith.

It didn't arrive in a dramatic collapse or a moment of conversion. I didn't cling to it out of desperation or as a last-ditch effort to be saved. It was already there – quiet, constant, like a thread woven through every season of my life. I didn't reach for it when things fell apart. It had been holding me all along.

We went to church every Sunday growing up. I remember trying not to laugh in the pews with my sister, stifling giggles behind folded hands while my mother and stepdad gave us sharp looks that said *enough*. It was a routine, a rhythm. I didn't question it. I went. Sat. Stood. Sang. Kneeled. Prayed. Believed.

My husband and I continued the tradition with our own kids. Sometimes out of rhythm, sometimes out of guilt, sometimes simply because it's what we did. But even when the practice felt routine, the presence of something greater never left me.

But when I got sober, something shifted. Faith stopped being a box to check on Sunday mornings. It became the heartbeat of my every day. When searching for support, I had gone to a couple of AA meetings, knowing they were rooted in faith. I'll never forget the warmth in those rooms, the trusted circle of once-strangers, bound by something deeper than words. The honesty. The humility. The grace. The deep faith. There was something deeply holy in the way people told the truth about their pain and still showed up with hope.

But I knew my path would look different. I wasn't called to a set structure or program. I was drawn to something quieter – more intimate. Something anchored in the faith that had quietly shaped my life since childhood.

Prayer, once reserved for Sunday mornings or moments of gratitude, became a guiding light – meeting me in the middle of the night when I couldn't sleep, whispering grace when cravings hit, offering steady ground when I felt like I was breaking. And it didn't sound polished or poetic. Most of the time, it was raw, almost childlike. *Help me. Hold me. Show me.* And somehow... He did.

In those early nights when I couldn't sleep – when the cravings hit like waves and I felt like I might drown – I'd whisper prayers in the dark, clinging to familiar verses like a raft, the kind I'd known since childhood: the Our Father, the Hail Mary. Words I didn't have to think about, just feel. When shame rose up in my throat like smoke, threatening to suffocate me, I gave it up. Not to my own willpower. But to something greater. I stopped gripping so tightly. I stopped trying to manage every emotion, every outcome, every corner of my pain. And slowly, I began to trust.

Maybe there was a plan I couldn't see. Maybe my brokenness wasn't the end of the story. Maybe, just maybe, I was being carried through it all. Week after week, I sat in church and listened as our pastor preached with a kind of quiet strength I clung to. I don't think he truly knew just how much I needed those sermons –

how often they landed like medicine. It felt, more times than not, as if he were speaking directly to me. As if God had handed him a note with my name on it. He reminded me that grace isn't earned. That redemption is always possible. That healing doesn't come through striving, but through surrender.

That connection deepened one Sunday during my niece's First Communion. As her godmother, I was honored to be part of the day by doing one of the readings at Mass – a small contribution to a moment that belonged to her. Afterward, Father Juan, our pastor, approached with kind eyes and a gentle, direct invitation: "Would you consider becoming a lector?" My stomach flipped. I felt a rush of nerves, completely caught off guard – and yet, something about it felt right. Like I was being nudged, not by chance, but by purpose. He didn't just offer a role – he extended trust, seeing a voice that could serve.

I went through the steps to make it official, and now, each month, I have the privilege of reading scripture aloud to our parish community. I usually tremble. I still take medication to steady the nerves that threaten to take over. But somehow, when I step up to the pulpit and begin to read, I feel something move through me – a calm that isn't mine. A presence that steadies me. I don't know if it's the Holy Spirit or simply grace, but whatever it is, I let it lead. I'm still learning to trust it. But what I know for sure is this: it is one of the greatest honors of my life.

Faith didn't fix everything. It didn't make the pain disappear or wrap my life in a tidy bow. But it gave me something to stand on when the ground beneath me crumbled. And sometimes, that's everything.

Sobriety has taught me just how fragile – and miraculous – life really is. But faith... faith has shown me I don't have to carry it alone. That even in my mess, I am seen. I am loved. I am held. My path didn't follow a program. It didn't come with a manual or a 12-step checklist. But it was mine. And God met me exactly where I was – in the trembling, in the quiet, in the undone. He still does.

Now, as a yoga teacher, I find myself in the presence of students and fellow instructors from all kinds of spiritual backgrounds – Jewish, Catholic, Muslim, Buddhist, spiritual but not religious, etc. And I find it beautiful. Not in spite of our differences, but because of them. There's something powerful in watching people root into something. Something greater. Something beyond the surface and deeper than the self.

Sometimes, people mistakenly believe that yoga itself is a religion. That assumption is understandable because yoga can feel deeply spiritual and often awakens something within that's hard to name. But yoga, at its core, does not require adherence to any specific belief system. It simply asks you to return – to your breath, your body, your presence. For me, yoga didn't replace my faith; it actually rooted me deeper in it.

We all call it different names, walk different paths, but I think we're all reaching for the same thing: love, connection, purpose, peace. To believe in something bigger than yourself – whatever you call it – is, in itself, a kind of prayer. A kind of surrender. And I've learned that it's not the labels that matter most. It's the way we show up. The way we trust. The way we keep reaching for the light, even in our darkest hours.

Faith grounded me in the present. It held me through sobriety, motherhood, marriage, and the unknown. But as the fog cleared and I finally began to see myself honestly – without filters, without numbing – I found myself asking not just what now, but how did I get here? Not to assign blame. Not to rewrite the past. But to understand it. To hold it with compassion. To offer grace to the little girl inside me who had been carrying so much, for so long.

Because healing doesn't just move forward. It loops back – inviting us to revisit the moments we thought we'd outgrown, and the questions we didn't yet know how to ask.

And eventually, it took me all the way to the beginning.

Chapter Nineteen

Wired This Way

It would be easy to look at that scene – the little girl alone on a plane, her body shaking with fear, no parent in sight – and say: Well, of course she ended up the way she did. Easy to cast blame. To say, she should never have been on that flight without her parents. To look for the mistake. To assign fault. To believe that if just one thing had gone differently, I might have grown up "normal."

I get it. Honestly, I've said those things to myself, too.

But here's the truth I've come to understand: It wasn't the flight. It wasn't the divorce. It wasn't a single moment.

I was predisposed to feel deeply. To fear deeply. To carry things in a way others might not. Something in me – my wiring, my chemistry, my spirit – was always going to bend toward sensitivity, toward anxiety, toward the need to make sense of a world that often felt too big, too loud, too fast.

Now, with time and perspective, I can say this with clarity: it wasn't the moment on the plane that broke me. The storm had started long before we took off. Something would have triggered it eventually. Maybe not that flight. Maybe not that year. Maybe not in childhood at all. But something. Because this wasn't just situational. This was part of me. Part of my makeup. My path. And sure, the circumstances shaped it. The pain added layers. The loneliness gave it form. But the root? The root had been there all along.

I can see all of that now. But back then, it was harder to hold. For a long time, I didn't just question my pain – I compared it. I'd look around at the world, hear stories on the news, see people navigating unimaginable losses, and think: *Who am I to feel this way? Why am I struggling so much when others have it so much worse?*

I used other people's suffering as a yardstick – a way to invalidate my own pain, to shame myself into silence. I told myself I should be able to handle it. That my life wasn't hard enough to warrant the chaos I felt inside. But that only pushed the pain deeper. It taught me to minimize, to dismiss, to pretend.

What I've come to understand is this: pain doesn't play by rules. It's not a contest. There's no scoreboard – no hierarchy of suffering. What breaks one person might barely touch another – and that doesn't make either experience less real. It took me a long time to learn that comparison doesn't just steal joy – it steals truth. It erases the subtle details that make our paths unique, flattens our stories into something small and tidy and false.

We all carry things. We all walk hard roads. And every path is worthy of compassion.

Healing brought with it a different kind of lens – one that let me see the past with more gentleness. I don't blame my parents. I know they were doing the best they could with the tools they had, in the time they were in. They were young. They were hurting, too – trying to untangle their own losses, deal with their own limitations, all while doing their best to raise two little girls caught in the middle of a life that no longer looked like the one they'd imagined.

There were no perfect choices. No perfect outcomes. But there was love. There was effort. There was care, even when it didn't look how I needed it to. And I've always known, even without words, that my mother carries guilt with her. The kind that lingers in quiet pauses and softened memories. I see it in the way she sometimes rewrites the past mid-sentence, as if she's still trying to make it right from a distance.

I've also come to understand this: my mother carries a powerful story of her own. I may not know all of it, but I've always felt its depth. I know that what she gave my sister and me wasn't modeled for her in the ways she needed. And still, she showed up. She mothered from a well that hadn't always been full – and yet, she poured. What she gave came from a place of intention, resilience, and love. I see that now. I honor it. And I carry a deep, quiet gratitude for all the ways she tried, even when it wasn't easy.

And maybe that's the heart of it – she gave us what she could, even when it cost her. That's something my sister and I have come to understand more clearly with time. We don't need her to rewrite anything. We don't want her to carry the weight of what-ifs. What we've always wanted is simple: her presence. Her laughter. Her full, unfiltered self. We know she did the best she could – with what she knew, with what she had – and that love was never lost on us. That effort never went unseen.

And now, as a mother myself, I've come to recognize that same ache – that quiet guilt that settles in when you love deeply and still fear you've gotten it wrong. I've looked at my children – especially my Olivia – and wondered what they'll carry from me. What I handed down without meaning to. For a long time, that guilt felt like too much to bear.

But I see it differently now. I've come to believe we're not here to be perfect mothers – we're here to be present. To stay. To keep showing up. To love out loud, not just in reflection. And maybe that's the heart of it – that steady, imperfect, unconditional love we offer our children... maybe that's always been enough.

With all the hindsight, heartache, and healing I now carry, I can finally see that this – all of this – was part of my path. The panic, the pain, the heartbreak, the bulimia, the drinking, the coming undone, the rebuilding... it all belonged.

Each piece has taught me something I never could have learned in a textbook or a therapy session or in a Sunday sermon. I have lived these lessons. Felt them in my bones – my aching, misunderstood bones. And I've risen from them. And that? That's something I would never trade. Because I know now – with every fiber of who I am – that there's purpose in the pain. That my story isn't just a mess to hide, but a message to offer. A map for others.

I've come to believe that God has been showing me the way all along. Even when I couldn't see it. Even when I wandered in the dark. Even when I mistook silence for absence. He was there. He is there. And now, the light I couldn't find for so long? I see it. I follow it. And when it dims, I wait. I breathe. I remember it always returns.

This path – winding and jagged and heartbreakingly beautiful – is mine. And I trust it now. I trust Him now. Because even if I was wired to struggle, I was also born to rise. And I am rising still.

And now, I get to carry that light into the rooms I'm honored and humbled to teach in. I get to remind others – and myself – that the struggle doesn't disqualify us. It deepens us.

Just like I tell my students at the end of class, as we lie still in that final quiet moment:

Let everything feel heavy.

VANESSA FRANCE

And then breathe into the lightness that always follows.

Because it does. It always, always does.

Chapter Twenty

Let Go

Which brings me back to where this all began: a frightened little girl on a plane, searching for safety in a world that felt anything but.

Back to that airplane seat. Back to the four-year-old girl with the tear-streaked cheeks and the white-knuckled grip on a plastic toy airplane. Back to the panic. The fear. The sense that no one was coming. That she was all alone – suffering in silence, long before she had words for her pain.

I see her so very clearly now.

I want to reach out and tuck a strand of hair behind her ear. I want to whisper, *You're going to be okay.* I want to tell her that life will not be easy – but it will be beautiful. That she'll hurt, and fall, and fight battles she never asked for – but she will rise. Again and again.

I want to tell her that it's okay to let go.

Let go of the toy airplane.
Let go of the illusion of control.

Let go of the belief that your worth is tied to your body, your behavior, your performance.
Let go of the shame. The secrecy. The self-doubt.
Let go of the bottle. Of the coping. Of the numbing.

Let go, and lean in.

Lean into the breath.
Lean into the present moment.
Lean into your faith.
Lean into the people who love you for exactly who you are – and trust that when you admit you're scared, when you ask for help, the ones who matter will meet you with support, not judgment.
Lean into the strength you don't know you have yet.
Lean into the practice. Into the healing. Into the truth of who you already are.
Lean into the truth that your body is not broken – it is a story. A map. A messenger.

That little girl didn't know then that her life would be messy and rich and sacred and real. She didn't know she'd battle bulimia and lose herself in wine glasses and sleepless nights. She didn't know that she'd feel unworthy, neglected, and sometimes broken.

She had no idea that one day she'd become a mother to four beautiful, wildly unique souls – that her love would multiply in ways that softened her and stretched her all at once. She didn't know peace would come – not by fixing everything, but by learning to sit still in the mess. That she'd find it again and again on a yoga mat, breath by shaky breath.

She didn't know she'd one day stand in front of others – not as someone who had it all figured out, but as someone willing to be real. To say, *I've been there.* To guide people back to themselves, not with answers, but with presence. To hold space the way others once held it for her. She didn't know she'd build something from the rubble – a space rooted in healing and truth and care.

She didn't know she'd survive. That the fear wouldn't swallow her. That the shame wouldn't last. That the story she was so afraid of would become her offering.

But I know that now.

And if I could hold her – that sweet girl unraveling midair, terrified and trying so hard to hold it together – I'd cradle her face in my hands, look deep into her eyes, and gently whisper through tears:

"Look at me..."

You made it.
You are safe now.
You don't have to do this alone anymore.
You can let go – not because you've failed, but because you've finally learned to trust something deeper.

Let go of the fear.
Let go of the weight.

You don't have to carry all of it anymore.

Come home.

To your breath.
To your body.
To your truth.
To your life.

And that is what I've done.

VANESSA FRANCE

Not perfectly, but fully.

Faithfully. Finally.

I let go – and finally trusted the One who carried me all along.

Afterword

This book was never meant to be written. Not because I didn't have a story to tell – but because for so long, I didn't believe it mattered. I didn't believe I mattered.

But over time – breath by breath, step by uncertain step – I began to reclaim the pieces I once tried to hide. I began to listen more closely to the voice I had buried beneath fear, shame, perfectionism, and survival. And that voice whispered something that changed everything: Tell the truth. It's time.

Unraveled isn't a manual. It's not a polished recovery story or a prescription for healing. It's simply my offering – one woman's journey through anxiety, disordered eating, addiction, faith, motherhood, and the long, nonlinear process of learning to come home to herself.

If something in these pages resonated with you – if you saw a piece of your own story reflected back – then I'm honored. That is why I wrote this.

May these words remind you that healing doesn't have to be loud to be holy. That we don't have to be perfect to be whole. And that the path forward is not paved with control – but with surrender, softness, and courage.

Thank you for walking beside me.

With love, Vanessa

Acknowledgements

Before I begin, I know this list is long – and that's the point. Healing doesn't happen in isolation. It happens when we let others in – when we allow ourselves to be seen, held, guided, and loved. Every name here is a thread in the fabric of this story – a reminder that I didn't walk this path alone.

To God – thank You for walking beside me through it all. For meeting me in the silence, the surrender, the unraveling – and for carrying me when I couldn't carry myself. This story is stitched with grace I didn't always recognize in the moment, but now see so clearly.

To my husband, Matt – thank you for loving me through every version of myself. For your steadiness, your belief in me, and your quiet strength. You saw me when I couldn't see myself. You gave me space to grow – and roots to stay grounded. I couldn't have done this without you.

To my children –
Maddie, my old soul. You have a quiet wisdom beyond your years, a humor uniquely your own, and a heart that holds more than it lets on. Your ambition and drive are fierce – and you inspire me every day with the way you move toward your dreams.
Lali, my light. You radiate joy and care so deeply it sometimes weighs heavy on your small shoulders. So much like me – in both the worry and the wonder. Thank you for your tenderness, your presence, and the way you remind me that

softness is strength.

Cam, my fire. You're a natural – a born athlete with a drive that humbles me and a spirit that shines, both on and off the ice. You're laid back and full of life, and your energy has always brought laughter and movement into our home.

Jack, my wonder. You experience the world in a beautifully unique way, and you've taught me more about presence, patience, and perspective than I could ever put into words. Your brilliance, your spirit, and your joy light up every room. You are each a chapter of this story. My why. My becoming. My home.

To Kaeli – you may not share our last name, but you share our hearts. Thank you for being such a constant in our lives – not just to Maddie, but to our whole family. You feel like one of our own.

To my sister, Mel – my first and forever friend. You have been there for me my whole life – through every season, every high and low, every quiet turning point. Thank you for your unwavering presence, your steady heart, and your love that never wavers.

To my niece Gianna and nephew Dylan – like my own children in so many ways. Thank you for teaching me about unconditional love, long before I fully understood it myself. You helped me know, deep down, that I was meant to be a mother.

And to my beautiful nieces, Annabelle Mae and Dani – your presence in my life is a joy and a blessing. You each hold a piece of my heart.

To my parents – thank you for loving me the best you knew how. This story holds both the ache and the grace, and I honor everything you gave.

Mom, I see the ways you tried – even when it wasn't easy – and I carry so much gratitude for the strength and softness you offered, especially in the moments when I needed it most. I love you just as you are – and always have.

To my stepdad, Dave – thank you for stepping in with presence and heart. For showing up consistently and loving me as your own.

To my dad – ours was a complicated story, but one that shaped me in deep ways. I carry your heart, your name through Jack, and the quiet faith that you're still with me.

To Barb – thank you for loving and caring for my dad the way you did. Your devotion and kindness meant more than words can ever express, and I will always be grateful for the way you stood by him.

To Nana – thank you for the love, the ice cream cones, the dancing, and the safety of your lake house. You left a mark on my heart that lives on in every "and that."

To Joyce and Ed – your love, your support, and your steady presence just next door have meant more than words can say. Thank you for being such an anchor for our family – your care has carried us through more than you know.

To our family on both sides – aunts, uncles, sisters-in-law, brothers-in-law and cousins – your steady, everyday love has carried us. Thank you.

To Rebekah and Timea – your friendship changed the course of my life. Thank you for dreaming big beside me, for holding sacred space, and for building something beautiful together. Zen isn't just a studio – it's a sanctuary, because of you.

To Queen – thank you for guiding me home to myself, one honest, messy truth at a time. The work you do as a therapist is sacred and powerful; your steadiness made courage possible.

To Teresa – for meeting me in one of the most tender, pivotal moments of my life and holding space with a kind of compassion I'll never forget. Your words gave shape to something I couldn't yet name. The mountain metaphor you offered lives in me now – a steady, sacred compass I will carry always.

To Coach Pic – thank you for being a steady voice during a season of quiet chaos. Your strength, consistency, and belief in me – even when I was struggling in silence – gave me something to hold onto. You may not have known the depth of what I was carrying, but your presence and your expectations helped anchor me when I needed it most.

To Jen – thank you for walking beside me in those early days of sobriety and faith. Our shared reflections and quiet texts helped carry me through more than you know.

To all my work colleagues (earlier in life and later) who became dear friends – thank you for being my safe place in the hardest seasons. I couldn't have made it through those times without you. You know how much you mean to me, though I'm not sure you'll ever know the depths. Erica, Montag, Sarah, Gerry and Anita – your support, laughter, and friendship carried me more than you'll ever realize.

To my childhood friends – thank you for loving me exactly where I was. You didn't know the depths of what I was carrying, but you knew more than most, and your laughter, loyalty, and steady presence gave me belonging when I needed it most.

To the friends who came later in life – thank you for meeting me where I was, for walking beside me through seasons of both breaking and rebuilding, and for reminding me that it's never too late to find true connection. Your friendship means more than I can say.

To all of the incredible instructors who have walked alongside me on this journey – thank you for your wisdom, your presence, and your heart. Each of you has influenced my path in meaningful ways, both on and off the mat. Especially Emily – your authenticity, grounded energy, and quiet strength have left an imprint I carry with me every day. I am endlessly grateful.

To Father Juan – thank you for your steady presence and for the wisdom you share week after week. Your homilies have helped ground me in grace, reminding me to look for God not just in the peace, but in the pain. Your words have deepened my faith and helped me return to what matters most.

To those who have walked beside Jack – the countless teachers, therapists, and guides who poured into him with such care – thank you. Especially Ms. Jamie, Ms. Karyn, and Ms. Shannan – your compassion, patience, and unwavering belief in him are gifts our family will never forget.

To every author, teacher, therapist, and soul who shared their stories before I could share mine – thank you for lighting the path.

To our Zen students – thank you for showing up on your mats with courage, vulnerability, and open hearts. You have reminded me, again and again, that healing is not a solitary path.

A heartfelt thank you to Paula, whose leadership and love created the original space that would eventually become Zen. Your work laid the groundwork for the community we're honored to nurture and grow today. We are forever grateful.

To my editor, Sheryl – thank you for your insight, guidance, and encouragement in shaping this book. Your wisdom and care helped me bring these pages to life, and I am so grateful.

And to every person who touched my journey in ways big and small – the friends and family who listened without judgment, the teachers who saw my children and met them with care, the hands that helped hold me up when I couldn't stand on my own – and to those I may not have named directly, please know this: your presence mattered. Your kindness mattered. This book is stitched with threads of grace, and it carries your imprint too.

With love and gratitude, Vanessa

Resources & Further Reading

If you're in immediate danger or thinking about harming yourself, call **911** (or your local emergency number).

Crisis & Support (U.S.)

988 Suicide & Crisis Lifeline – Call or text **988**, chat at 988lifeline.org
Crisis Text Line – Text **HOME** to **741741** (crisistextline.org)
SAMHSA National Helpline (substance use & mental health) – **1-800-662-HELP (4357)**
NAMI HelpLine (mental health information & support) – **1-800-950-NAMI (6264)**, nami.org/help
ANAD Eating Disorders Helpline – **(888) 375-7767**, anad.org

Postpartum Support International (perinatal mood/anxiety) – **1-800-944-4773**, postpartum.net

Outside the U.S. – See **Befrienders Worldwide** (befrienders.org) for international crisis centers.

Books Mentioned in This Memoir

Alcohol, Sobriety & Recovery:
This Naked Mind – Annie Grace
We Are the Luckiest – Laura McKowen
Quit Like a Woman – Holly Whitaker
Blackout: Remembering the Things I Drank to Forget – Sarah Hepola
The Sober Diaries – Clare Pooley
The Easy Way to Stop Drinking – Allen Carr
Recovery 2.0 – Tommy Rosen
The Sober Survival Guide – Simon Chapple

Anxiety, Neuroscience & Healing:
Rewire Your Anxious Brain – Catherine M. Pittman & Elizabeth M. Karle
Rewired – Erica Spiegelman

Memoir & Becoming:
Between Breaths: A Memoir of Panic and Addiction – Elizabeth Vargas
The Highlight Real – Emily Lynn Paulson
Untamed – Glennon Doyle

How to Use These Resources
If you're here, you're not alone. Start small – choose one book that tugs at you (education, memoir, tools). Read at your own pace, underline what lands, and bring it into conversation – with a support group, a trusted friend, or a therapist. Keep the crisis numbers somewhere easy to reach – in your phone, on the fridge, in your bag. Most of all, be gentle with yourself: one page, one step, one breath at a time.

Reader Reflection

Take a breath. Place your hand over your heart. And ask yourself: What am I ready to let go of?

Unraveled was written not just to tell my story – but to invite you to reflect on yours. You don't have to have lived through the same details to recognize the ache of anxiety, the pull of perfectionism, the silence of shame, or the long road back to yourself.

You are not broken. You are becoming.

If something here stirred something in you – write about it. Pray about it. Move your body. Cry. Talk to someone you trust. Come back to your breath. Start where you are.

Healing isn't a destination. It's a relationship – with yourself, with others, with grace. And you are already on the path.

Prompts to consider:

– What have I been carrying that I'm ready to lay down?

– Where in my life have I mistaken control for safety?

– What would it feel like to trust my body – not as a problem, but as a messenger?

– Who can I be honest with – today, right now?

VANESSA FRANCE

– Where is grace already showing up in my story?

Thank you for reading. Thank you for feeling. Thank you for staying. Take one more breath. Loosen your grip. Let go – and begin.
The unraveling is where your story truly begins.

Notes

This space is yours – for whatever rises. Write what stirs you. Name the memories. Speak the prayer. Set the intention. Start small – one page, one step, one breath at a time.

VANESSA FRANCE

UNRAVELED

VANESSA FRANCE

UNRAVELED

VANESSA FRANCE

About The Author

Vanessa France is a writer and yoga teacher who helps people breathe a little deeper and tell the truth about their lives. As co-founder of Zen Yoga & Wellness, she creates spaces – on the mat and in community – where unraveling isn't failure; it's the beginning.

For years, Vanessa tried to be small, quiet, and "good." Anxiety hummed, perfectionism pressed in, and alcohol promised relief. Recovery taught her something different: honesty is a practice, tenderness a strength, and healing happens one breath at a time. *Unraveled* is the story that unfolded as she found her way back – and the invitation she offers to others.

A mother of four, Vanessa writes in the margins of real life – juggling rides for the kids' sports and school, teaching yoga classes, walking with her husband and Gracie, summers in Vermont, and Sunday dinners with the crew. She loves early mornings with coffee, paddleboarding on still water, and the steady presence of her faith.

Through Zen Yoga & Wellness, Vanessa leads classes, workshops, and retreats that weave nervous-system–friendly practices with accessible breathwork, gentle strength, and rest. This book is her offering beyond the studio – a reminder that anxiety, addiction, and struggle do not mean you are broken. They are part of becoming.

VANESSA FRANCE

Website – vanessafrance.com

Follow – instagram.com/zenyogaandwellness & facebook.com/zenyogaandwellness

Classes & retreats – zenyogandwellness.com

Connect – zenyogaandwellness@gmail.com